# BRIDGES

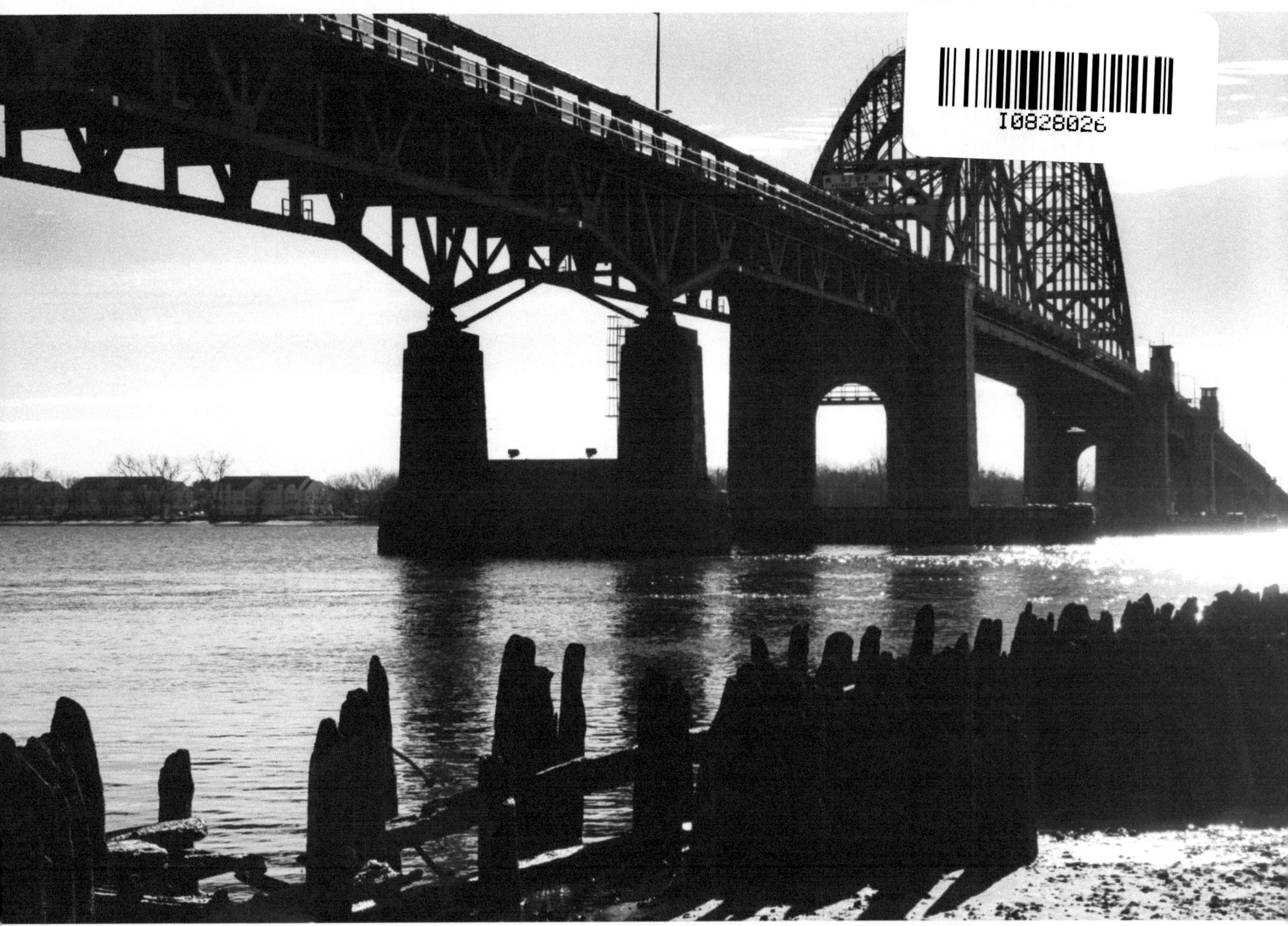


An Artist's Roadside Journey
through America's Steel Spans

*Volume 2. Mid-Atlantic*

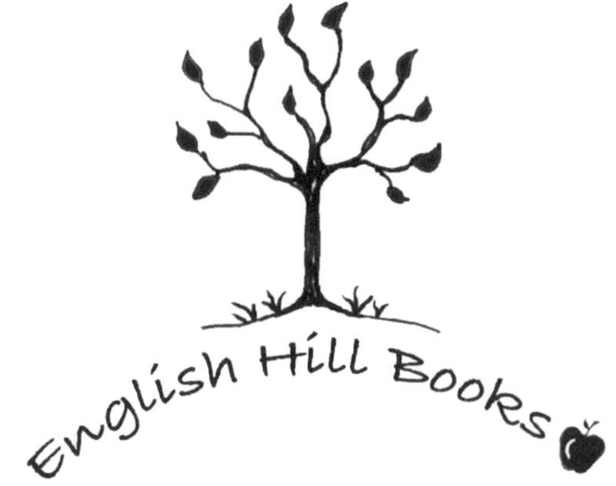




First Printing 2023
Edited by Erroll Imre

I dedicate this book to
my father, Leslie A. Grimord,
who never tried to keep me from
chosing art as my profession.

Art chose me,
not the other way around.
My rational self would never have done so.

# Acknowledgments

In Volume 1 of ***Bridges,*** I have an incomplete list of acknowledgments that pertain to this entire three-volume project. I will briefly mention the names cited there and then use Volume 2 to add to the list of people I believe helped or guided my path as a photographer of bridges.

My wife, Joan, deserves many thanks for putting up with me and helping with publishing issues. My daughter, Monique, has valuable design expertise that will continue to guide me through this project. Robert Asman, deceased, was my chemical photography go-to guy for decades and freed me from the necessity of having my own darkroom. I was already up to my neck in sculpture studio machinery and camera equipment and was happy to not spend the time and money building and supplying one. Finally, I wish to remind readers of the two great websites that pertain to bridges: ***HistoricBridges.org*** and ***Bridgehunter.com***. Both sites have comprehensive lists of bridges that continue to grow, as well as a wealth of photographs and data that will hopefully increase awareness of these structures' importance. A significant portion of the physical anthropology of the Industrial Age is recorded in our bridges, and losing them to dynamite and wrecking balls is tantamount to book burning.

Now, I wish to add some additional acknowledgments to the ones I carried over from Volume 1. David Plowden is a photographer and archivist of industrial things as they disappear from the American landscape. Born in 1932, he beat me by a generation in following an interest in scenes of the Machine Age. His book titled ***Bridges: The Spans of North America***, first published in 1974, ignited my interest in taking pictures of bridges. I bought my copy at Hacker Art Books on 57th Street in New York in 1981, under its original Viking Books publisher. It cost me $55, which was a massive deal for me. The book has since been republished under other well-known imprimaturs and is still available today, along with a long list of other titles that dwarfs anything I'll accomplish as a photographer. However, I get shoulders to stand on.

Another hero of photography is Timothy H. O'Sullivan (1840-1882). He was a photographer for Clarence King's 1867 geological survey of western North America. His pictures are famous and widely published, so my interest in his work points to nothing unique about me, nor is his influence on my work idiosyncratic or of any particular effect. I simply like his forthrightness of style in how he pointed his camera. "I'm here, and that's over there, and I'm gonna photograph it," is how I imagine him encountering his subjects. He's an antidote to a world that tries too hard.

I'll finish this batch of acknowledgments by mentioning a friend from my college years, Erroll Imre. We were roommates for our junior and senior years and shared an interest in photography. We would sometimes walk the streets of Albion, Michigan, with our cameras and snap pictures of things we happened upon. One day he announced his newly minted plans of going to law school instead of engineering. I told him it was a bad idea. Almost 50 years later, he claims he wished he had listened to me. I was probably correct, but I got an editor out of the deal. Long after quitting his law career, he went into editing and then later offered to help me and my wife navigate the wordsmith's art for self-publishing. He's been of incalculable value to us. Thank you, Erroll!

## Introduction

Welcome to Volume 2 of ***Bridges: An Artist's Roadside Journey through America's Steel Spans.*** In Volume 1, we looked at bridges in and around Pittsburgh and ended in the distant outskirts, on the edge of commuting distance. Volume 2 picks up the journey on the Allegheny River in Armstrong County, from where we continue into the thinly populated northwest corner of Pennsylvania. Next, we cross into New York and look at a couple of bridges in Niagara. From there, we jump into the Mid-Atlantic region proper, where we thoroughly study the Chesapeake Bay waters as they narrow and become the grand and primordial river called the Susquehanna. With its primary and west branches, this river takes us back and forth between Appalachia and the Mid-Atlantic and goes northward to its headwaters in New York State.

The survey becomes more urban after leaving the Susquehanna River system and begin journeys that include the Hudson's East River in NYC, the Delaware and Lehigh Rivers, and a quick stop on the Raritan River in New Jersey. Philadelphia, our home for 24 years, figures heavily at the end of the book. I wish more time was spent in NYC, but the 9/11 attacks on the Twin Towers made me nervous about hanging around NYC bridges, and subsequent anecdotal information supported my concerns. In fact, it was only after 9/11 that I spoke to someone with a badge, and usually, but not always, the conversation went well. Gone are the days when artists and intellectuals could walk across battle lines with tacit safe passage. Yes, it was so in my life and past periods of history, and I mean this in both literal and figurative terms. I miss those times, and I doubt I, or our children, will experience anything like it in the future.

Bridges and the areas underneath bridges, railroad tracks, rivers, abandoned industry, and remote roadways are no man's lands, places outside the law, so to speak. Simultaneously peaceful and sometimes dangerous, these are ungoverned enclaves on the edge of the structured world. These places share nothing with society, whether adjacent to farmland or a city. To a small minority of people, such images wake them up, and I'm not sure why. As I fill these volumes, I'm reflecting on this question, which doesn't need an answer; I will follow the abandoned railroad tracks over the soft ocher-color grass into the forested undergrowth no matter what. It's what I do.

## Purchasing Photographs

Prints of my photographs are available for purchase by contacting me through our publishing company website: ***englishhillbooks.studio*** or directly with my email address: ***pgrimord@gmail.com***. Identify each image with the book volume number, page number, and the associated eight-digit archive number. Prices are quoted on request.

Philadelphia is called the "City of Neighborhoods," and that it is. Navigating such a place is easy once you know the social geography and what's expected of the traveler when crossing from one neighborhood into another. Perhaps what isn't well understood is how the entire Mid-Atlantic region is like that; there are informal lines of demarcation all over the place. When my wife, Joan, and I moved to the East Coast from the Industrial Midwest, we picked up on the various social/cultural customs during everyday encounters. We both seemed blessed with a high natural social anthropology. We began adjusting to where we happened to be standing, primarily by doing nothing more than realizing where we were.

Of course, many people will say this happens everywhere, and it does. I'm suggesting it's a matter of degree which makes the Mid-Atlantic distinctive. For instance, New York City is more than a city; it's its own city-state. Crossing the Hudson is entering a different country. The same can be said of Washington, D.C., except, in this case, the Beltway surrounding the District is the line of demarcation. Baltimore is nothing like D.C., Philly, Wilmington, Allentown, or anyplace else I've been in the Mid-Atlantic. These distinctions extend beyond cities, too. The Commonwealth of Pennsylvania is a crazy quilt of regional expressions; stumbling into new colloquialisms, food eccentricities, or "styles of being" are expectable when making only a short day trip. Crossing the Delaware River into New Jersey requires a specific prep time, with traffic only part of the reason. It is a place very different from PA, and that's before noticing the difference between North Jersey and South Jersey. Connecticut gives me a vague feeling I'm intruding into something; I think all of New England is that way. In Upstate New York, I can breathe and Joan and I like it up there, but it resembles no place in Pennsylvania and has nothing in common with New York City.

We currently live in the eastern part of Central Pennsylvania. Traveling east from our home takes us into Northeast PA, which is decidedly part of the Mid-Atlantic; go west, and we're in Appalachia. We live on the line between these two distinct mega-regions. I sub-titled Volume 2 Mid-Atlantic and left out Appalachia because the latter is more extensive and spreads to areas outside the purview of this book. However, we will repeatedly be crossing back and forth over this line during this adventure. The cultures of these two regions couldn't be more different, which I will summarize: The Mid-Atlantic looks eastward, over the Atlantic Ocean, to something or anything not native to America. Appalachia looks not westward but inward, to something not recognizable by anyone outside their world. The outcomes couldn't be more distinct. My purpose isn't to propose an ethnographic thesis. Instead, I wish to present to my readers a general stage on which this adventure happens; my photographs trace an *artist's* journey, and context is everything.

The 24 years we spent in Philly were in a marginal neighborhood in almost all respects. It was a wasteland not of the T.S. Eliot sort; it never developed that far, which was its charm. The area gentrified, and we left for the countryside. I took with me a stack of black+white photographs accumulated while traveling up and down the Northeast Corridor. After the move, the easy proximity of remote stretches of rivers and railroad tracks made photographing bridges more accessible than ever. And from our old Philly neighborhood, I brought my tolerance of lost humanity, sharpening my eye for bridges by following the hinterlands, the edgy areas loosely tethered to modernity. So, let's get started.

The Kittanning Bridge, pictured on Page 3, is a well-preserved span in a similarly maintained Pennsylvania small town on the banks of the Allegheny River. The town's streets and shops seem better off than what is usually found in the PA outback, and a local church displayed a lawn plaque drawing attention to its Tiffany stained glass windows.

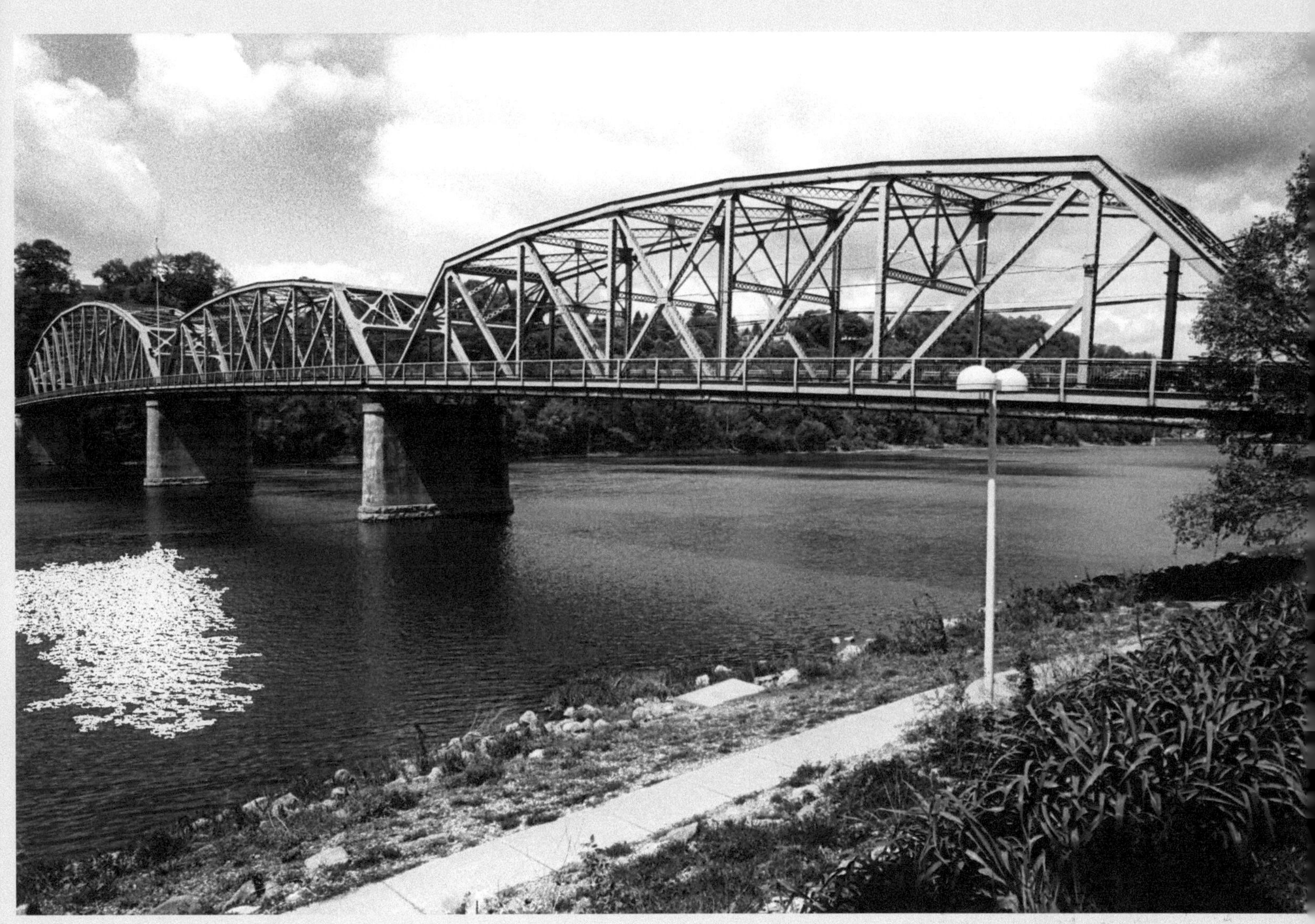

13-4759-06

Front Cover 12-4639-03

Inside Cover 13-4818-13

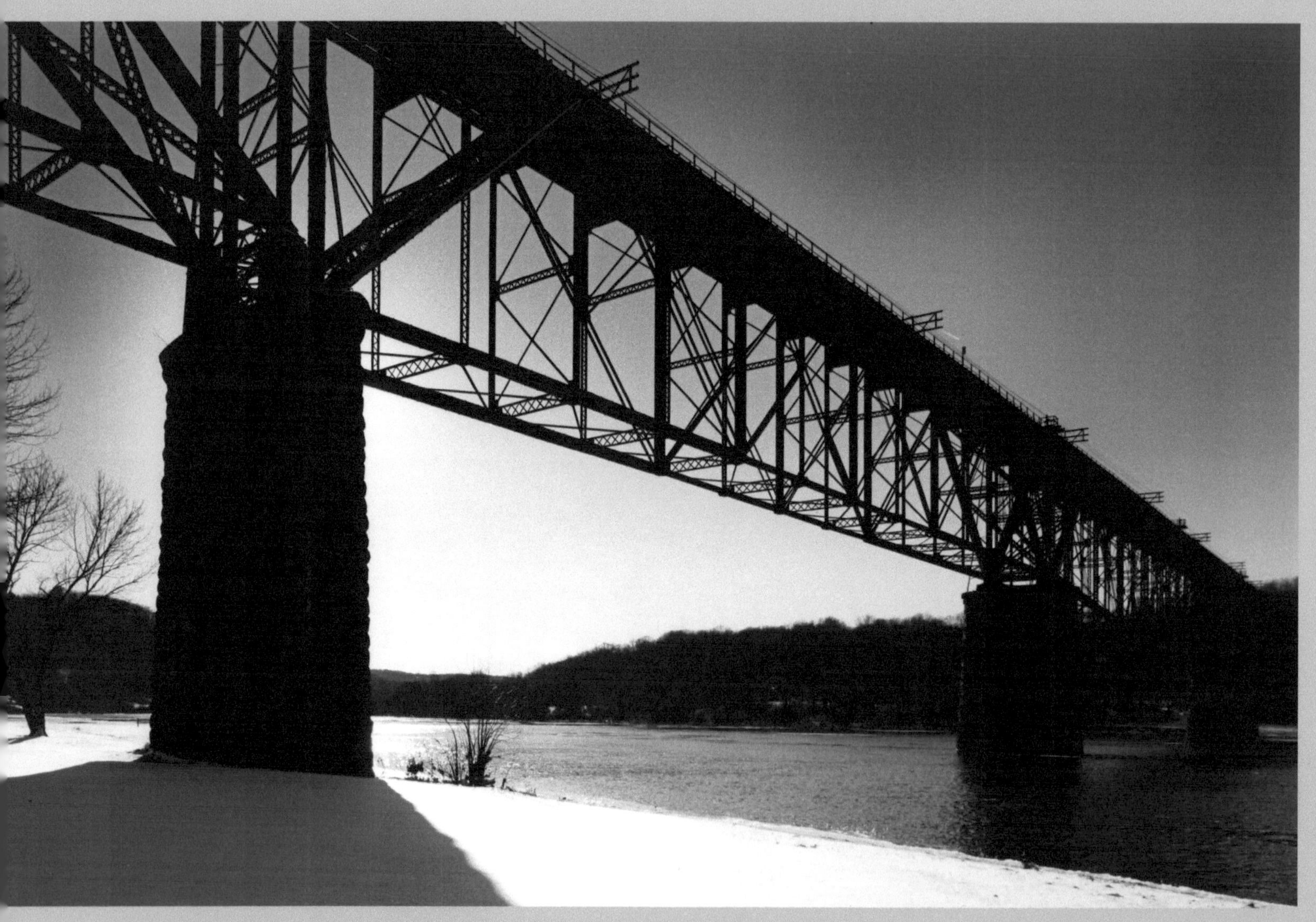

14-4829-27

4.

On page 4 is pictured the Mosgrove Railroad Bridge. When I first encountered it, its towering majesty took my breath away. I didn't know it was coming as I drove around a bend in the road running alongside the Allegheny River. They say it's exceptionally sturdy in design and construction; it will probably be with us for many years.

Aiming my camera into the sun and getting a good photograph is challenging. The Mosgrove Bridge is such a picture, and I like how it turned out. Obviously, the sun is behind the pier, which is one way to solve the problem. The photograph on the front cover is a second example; it shows the Northampton Street Bridge in Easton, PA, on the Delaware River. And the inside cover has a third "shooting-into-the-sun" photo, this one of the Tacony-Palmyra Bridge which is located on the Delaware River in Philadelphia. Both of these bridges will be discussed further as we visit these places.

With the cloudless sky in the background, the lighting in the Mosgrove photo provides sharp definition of the truss members that carry the tracks high above the river. Thick and thin members crisscross to create a steel dance that confounds gravity. Bridges are magical, and I need to re-introduce two concepts discussed in Volume 1 that unmask the trick, namely, the forces of *tension* and *compression*. These things occur in practically everything and are consciously controlled in bridge design and construction. Long story short, tension forces pull apart, and compression pushes together, like muscle tissue pulling against bone. We stand and pick up things the same way a bridge holds itself up and carries vehicles.

With bridges, particularly antique designs, tension elements often look sinewy and are sometimes made with cable or chain-linked parts. Compression elements are thick and stiff and built up with rivets and lattices. The Mosgrove photo clearly shows these things as defined by the variable thicknesses in the steel members. Also, tension elements are often placed diagonally and form "V"s, "X"s, and triangles inside the truss configuration. In the pages ahead, we will revisit these bridge forces and put them into some sort of order.

***A note about the text:*** *I am not a bridge designer or engineer; I'm an artist fascinated with bridges and a sculptor who works with bridge design principles. So, my understanding of bridge engineering arrives via a hands-on studio practice enformed through intuition; no classroom understanding of physics accompanies me on my bridge travels. My explanation of how bridges work is a formulation of words and images that match exactly how I figured out these things; indeed, I'm learning about bridges as I write these words and contemplate my phrasing. I'm inviting readers to join me in discovering steel spans with the eyes of a curious artist and a penchant for roaming the country under open skies.*

A short walk north along the Allegheny River from the Mosgrove Bridge is the Templeton Bridge, also called the Buffalo and Pittsburgh Allegheny River Railroad Bridge. I'll go with the first designation; it's less wordy. Pictured on page 7, this bridge is called a *Pennsylvania through truss*, which refers to the design pattern that guides the tension and compression forces operating across the spans.

Until now, I've avoided referring to the various truss designs because the discussions can get arcane and wordy. In Volume 1, I simply called all of them a *truss* or a *simple truss*. In Volume 2, this won't work because we will visit numerous simple truss bridge configurations due to the nature of the Mid-Atlantic waters. The Susquehanna River, in particular, is heavy with trusses, i.e., the classic simple truss bridges people associate with railroad spans. I strongly urge my readers to refer to the website, ***HistoricBridges.org***, and receive a thorough education on bridge design, especially looking at the part that deals with trusses. Nathan Holth runs the website and is passionate about bridges and their preservation. Scroll and find his essay, *Introduction to Historic Bridges*. This will make understanding some of my discussions easier, and he will cover all the various truss configurations with pictures and arrows.

Some may ask why I would bother with a book about bridges after discovering the completeness and comprehensiveness of Nathan Holth's work? I'm coming to the topic with black+white film photography being the primary focus of intent. I love bridges, but I love black+white photography even more, and with digital's replacement of film, analog images are becoming prized. I'm writing these books on bridges to be remembered as a collector of pictures with a personal interest in bridges, not the other way around.

***A note on viewing my photographs:*** *The printing paper used in these pages could be brighter and dulls the tonal subtleties in my black+white photos. I was aware of this before publication and managed the images accordingly. Please view these pages under intense indoor or natural outdoor light; this will significantly increase the perceived complexity in grayscale tones. I shot these pictures with 400 ISO Kodak Professional Film, Tri-X, and T-Max. Both are forgiving films for subjects presenting broad and unpredictable light conditions. I'm fully aware and approve of the inherent graininess of these films; a gritty look on a gritty subject is appropriate. Also, I applied a 25% sepia-tone overlay to each photograph to give the book a slightly antique feel.*

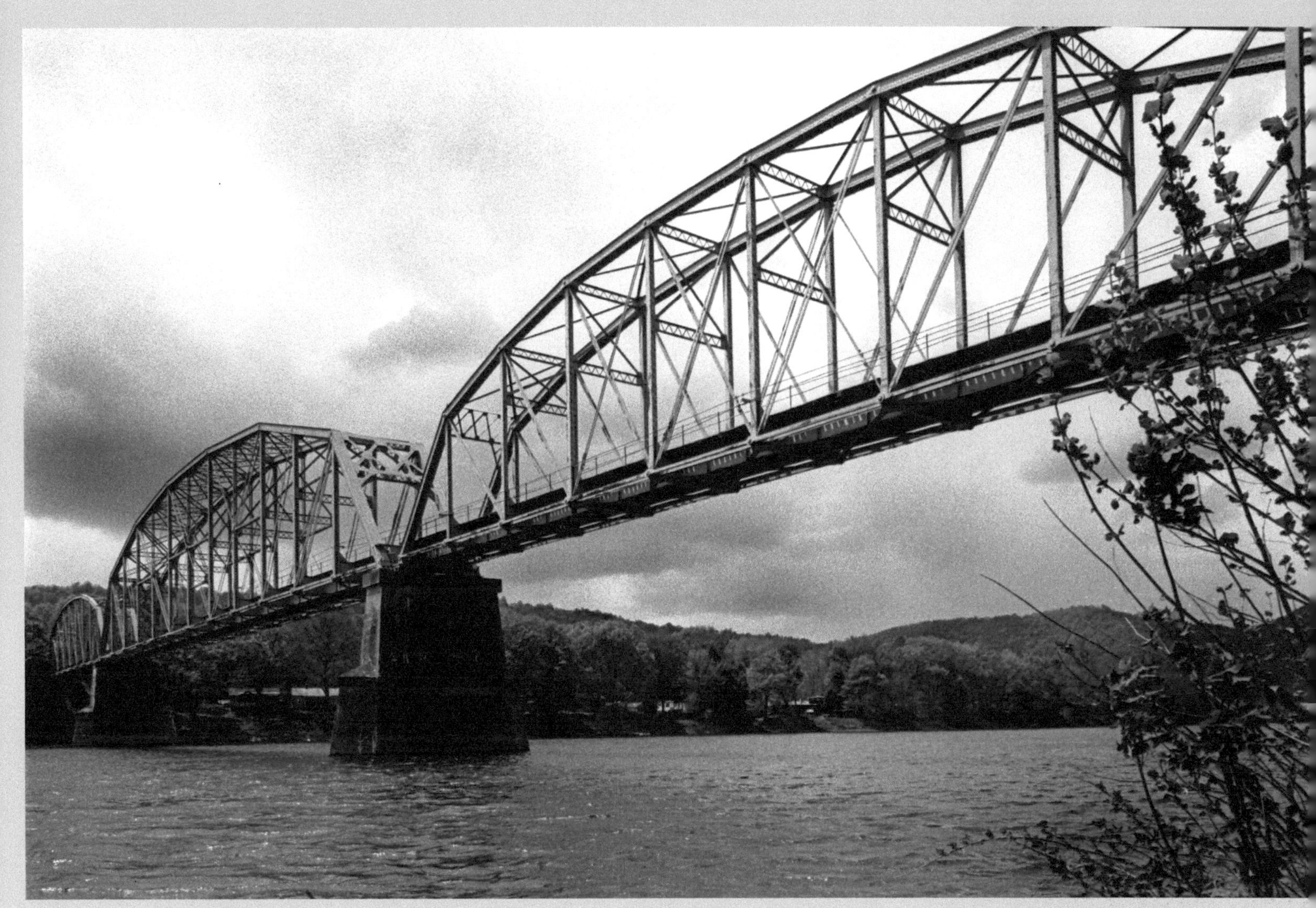

13-4757-32

The Parker Bridge is pictured on page 9. The configuration is called a *Parker* truss, which sports an arch-shaped top chord. Another feature is how the diagonal members are placed to “V” toward the bottom/center, making an “X” where they meet. I will make passing references to these distinctions throughout this volume. By the way, the Parker Truss is not related to the Parker town name where this specimen is located. It’s worth noting how the area around Parker has a desolate beauty that is unique to the western slope of the Allegheny Mountains. This feature continues as we travel north into the Pennsylvania oil region and New York State.

In 1979, my brother was married in Jamestown, NY, on Lake Chautauqua. I went there with my bicycle in the trunk so I could take day trips during my stay. I recall pedaling south into Pennsylvania and being knocked over by the subtle yet distinct attraction to the land and atmosphere; I will never forget this. I was sensing something in the transition zone between the Allegheny Mountains and the plains of Ohio; it’s a special place that isn’t widely recognized. Maybe I should shut up to keep it that way.

The picture on page 10 captures what I’m talking about.

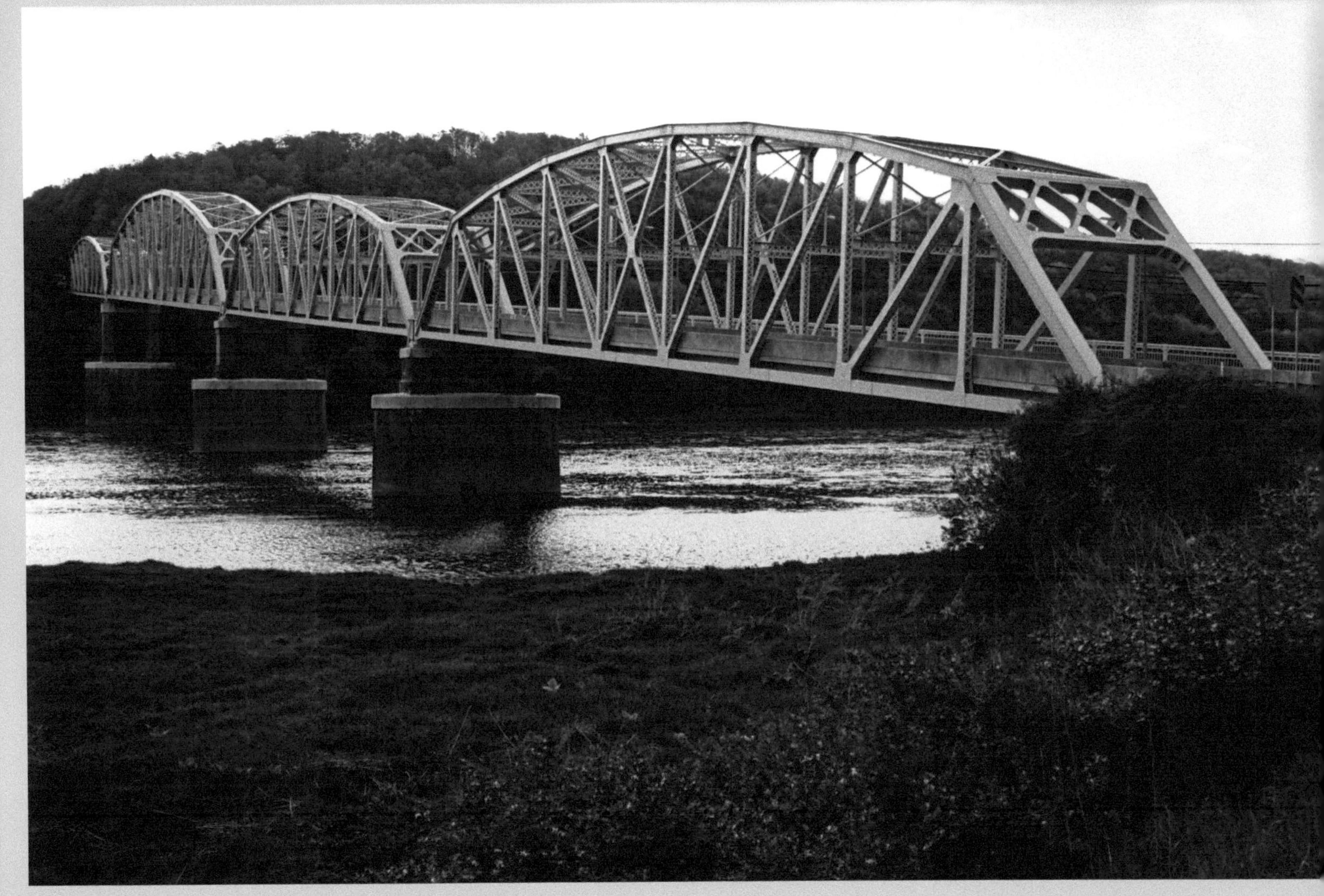

13-4758-04

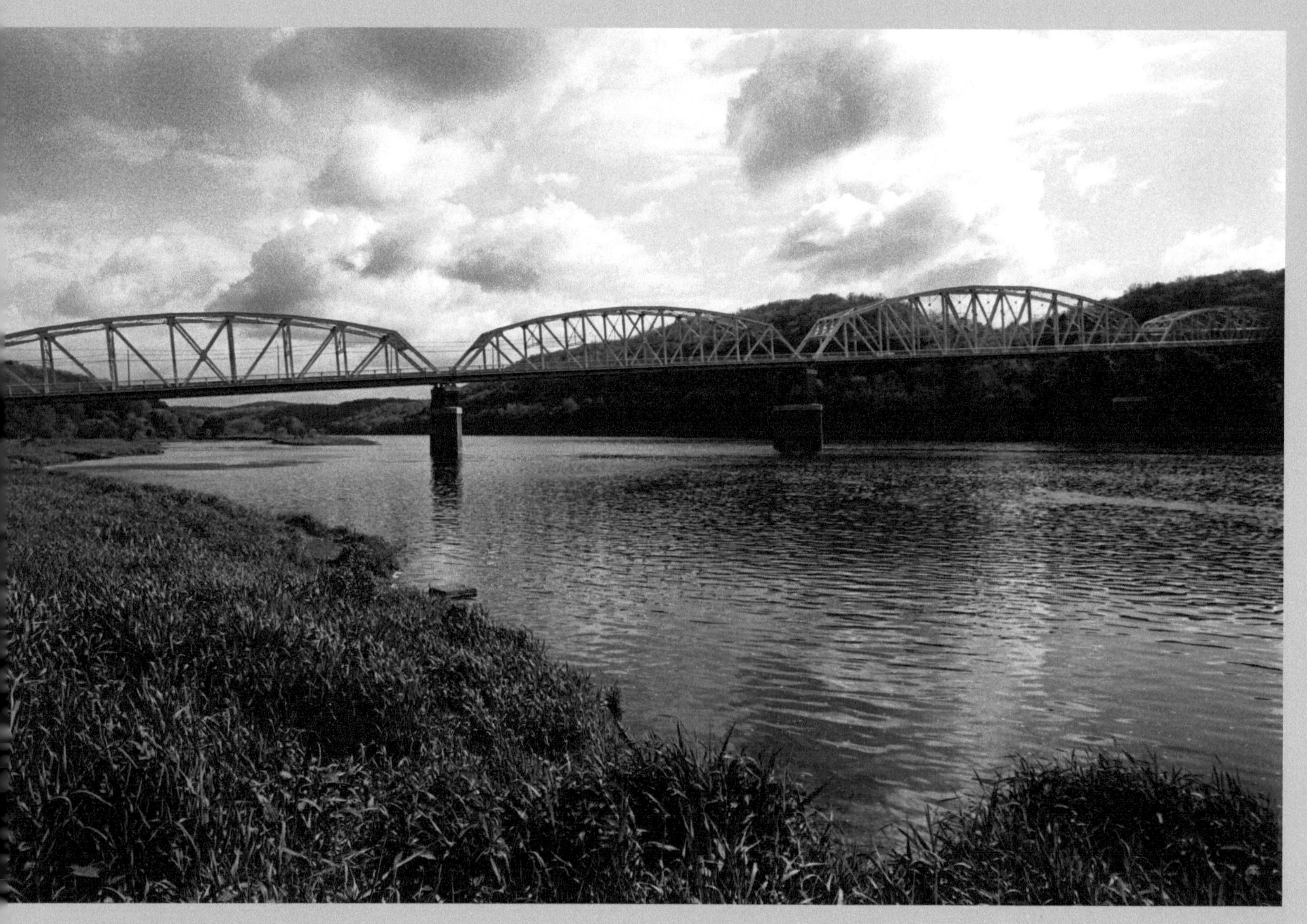

13-4756-23

13-4748-21 Overleaf

The Parker Bridge is built on a profoundly sloping grade. This isn't something I usually notice or look for when visiting a bridge due to its rarity. It's possible I became conscious of this feature only after looking at my photograph of the bridge. The main span of the McKees Rocks Bridge in Pittsburgh, covered in Volume 1, has a famous slope cleverly incorporated into the design, which is best discerned by measuring the difference in the end columns. It's subtle but visible.

On the overleaf, pages 12+13, is the Hunter Station Bridge, and it recently bit the dust courtesy of our road planners. The photo was taken in 2013 and was left ignored by me because I couldn't remember where along the Allegheny River that I found this bridge; I only knew there was a golf course or park acreage off to one side of the bridge. It's where I parked. I scanned up and down the Allegheny River using Google Earth and found the bridge by locating the recreational acreage. Unfortunately, a new bridge was under construction alongside the Hunter Station Bridge, so in real time, the old bridge was already gone, or soon-to-be.

The Hunter Station Bridge configuration is called a *Pratt* truss and is like a *Parker* truss with a flat upper chord instead of an arched one. Both types of trusses have diagonal members "V" toward the bottom/center of each span; note how the "V"s meet and overlap to make "X"s in the middle.

I printed this bridge on two pages and had to crop out some lovely reflections in the river beneath the bridge; I wanted to accentuate the bridge, but it came at a cost.

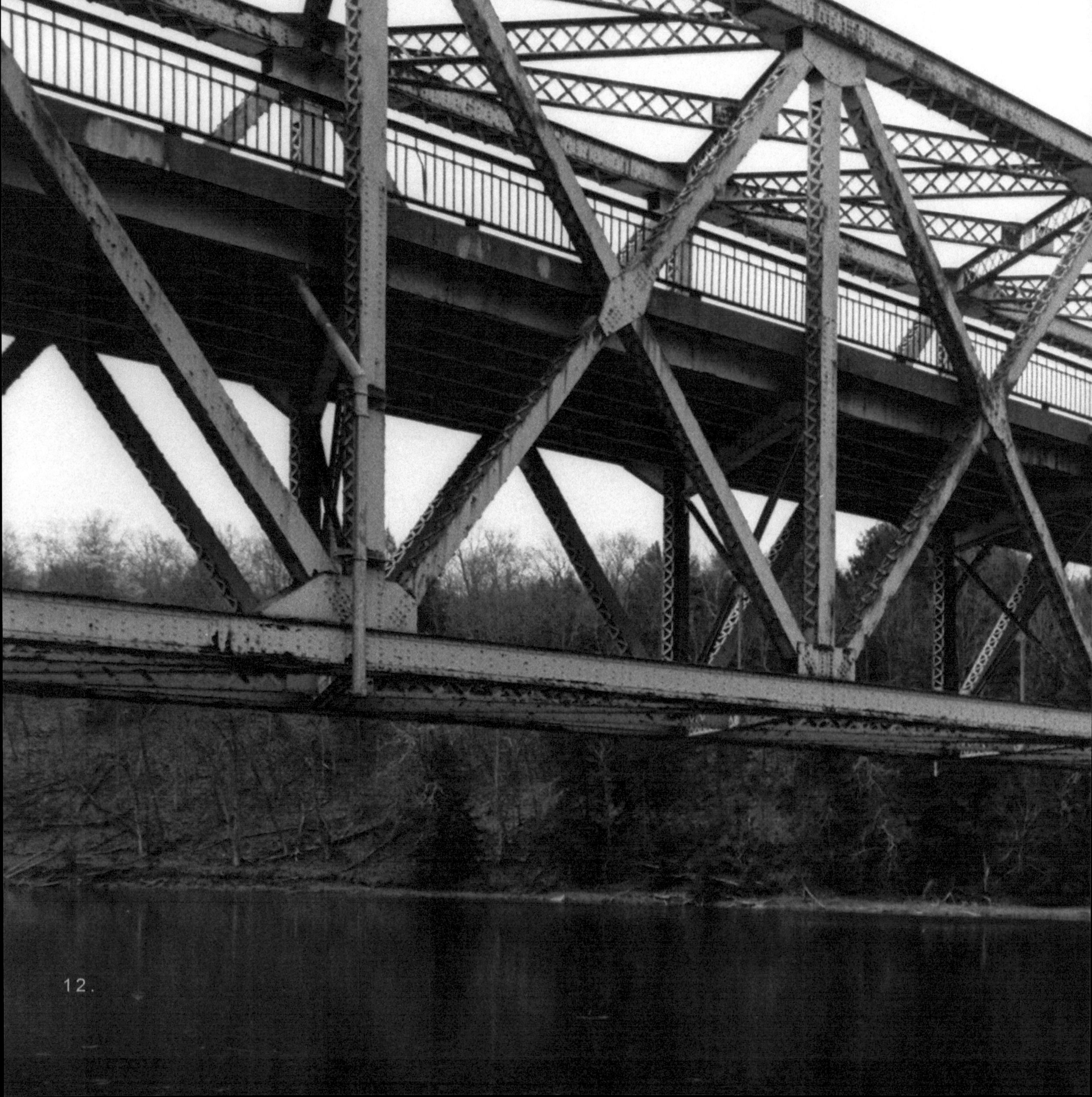

12.

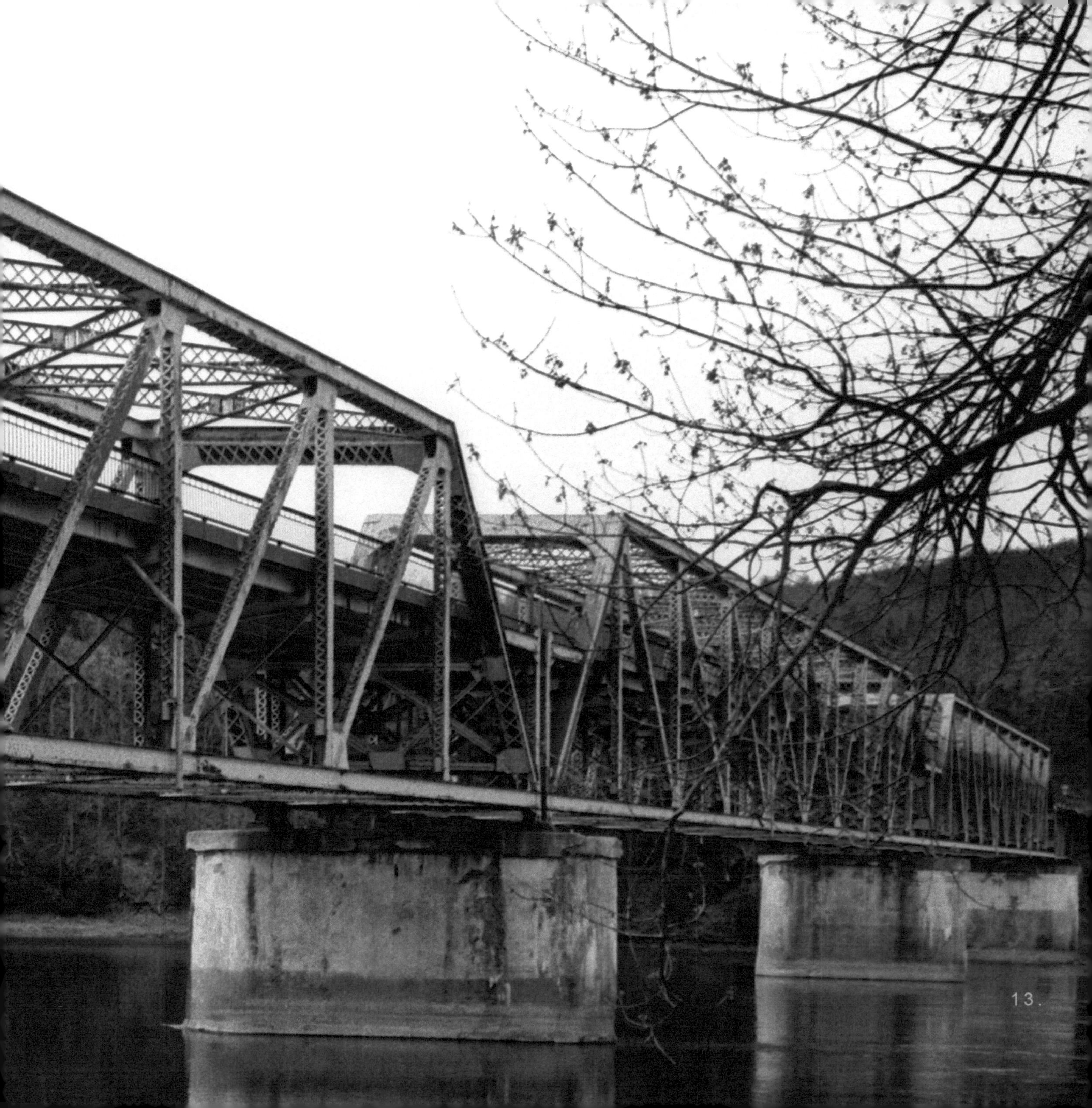

13.

As with the Hunter Station Bridge, the bridge on page 15 required a Google Earth search because I incorrectly logged it as belonging to Oil City, PA. It's in a town called Tidioute, where my wife and I enjoyed lunch looking out the Victorian windows of an empty restaurant. The time-forgotten towns of northwestern PA have an antiquarian sameness that both of us notice and appreciate.

The oil industry began in this region and was later left behind as larger oil fields were discovered. Somewhere, I read that the oil pumped from the ground was of such refinement that it could almost go straight into your car engine's crankcase. And a clear residue that gathered on the pumps and bottoms of oil drums was discovered to have skincare value and came to be called Vaseline. Today, there are few signs of the early Machine Age hustle and bustle that filled these hills. Every year, Joan and I pass through the region on an art voyage to western New York and the Chautauqua Institution. We like it out there.

The Tidioute Bridge is a two-span *Parker* truss crossing the Allegheny River; the diagonals "V" toward the bottom/center, and the top is arched. Going cross-eyed trying to discern what I'm describing is made worse by how the "V"s turn into "X"s as they cross over each other in the center. The middle of each truss is where the most significant tension and compression energy occurs, so overlapping the geometry makes good sense.

Pages 16+17 have another view of the Tidioute Bridge.

Next, we leave Pennsylvania for Upstate New York and the Niagara region. The western side of New York has more in common with my native state of Michigan than anything Mid-Atlantic or Appalachian. New York is a Great Lakes state, lost in the shadows of Manhattan skyscrapers and 20 million people.

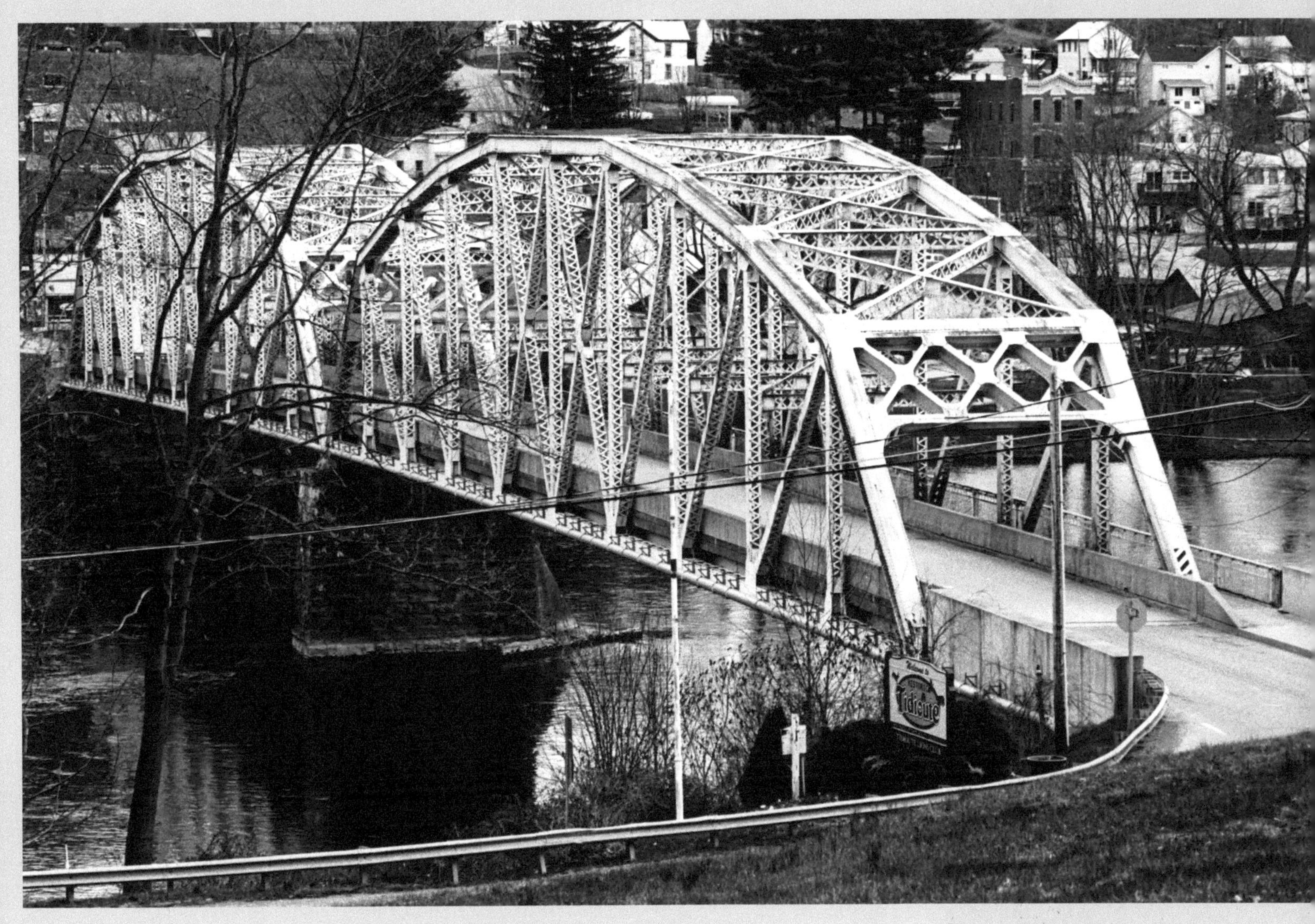


13-4746-25

Overleaf 13-4748-28

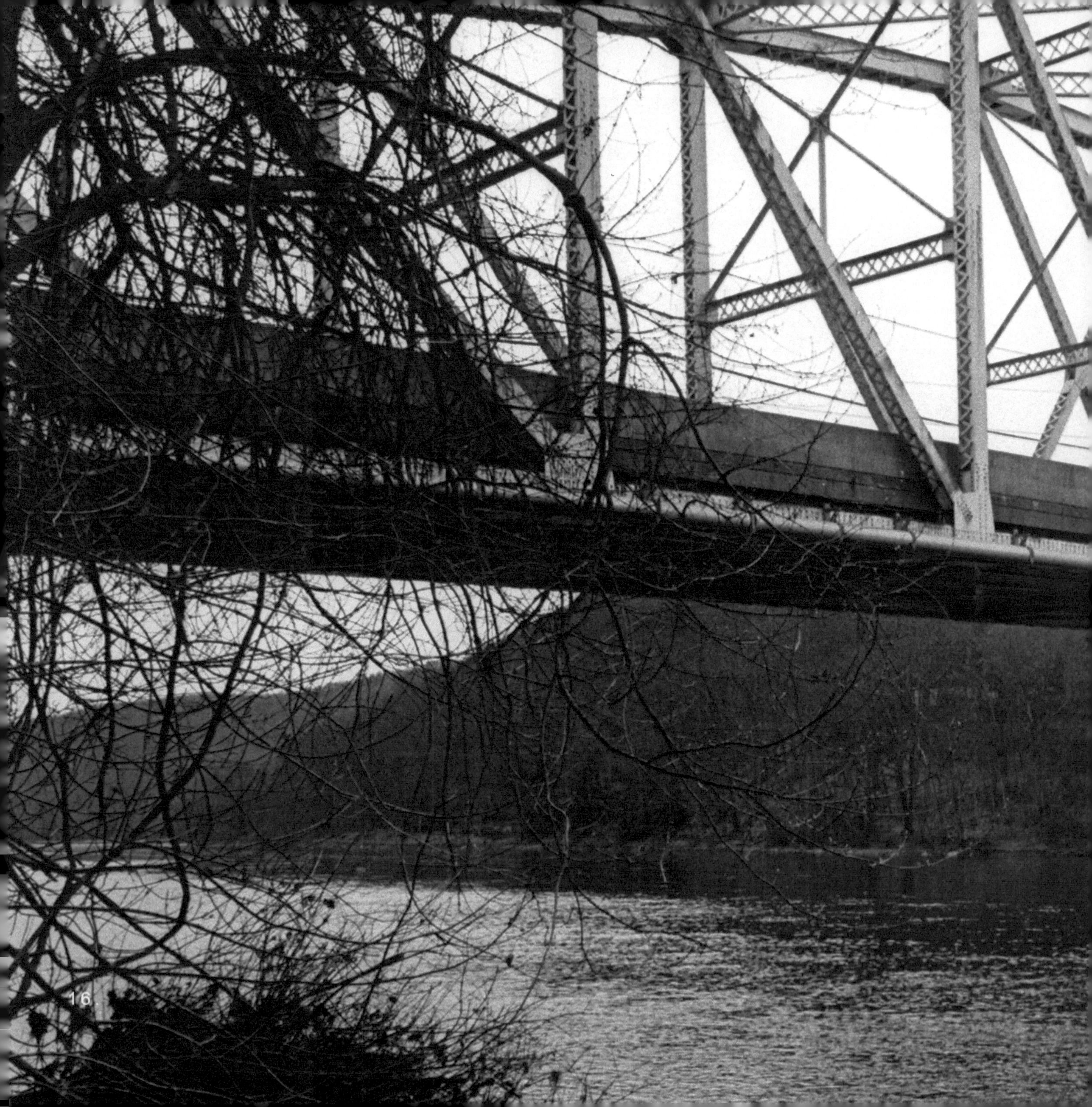

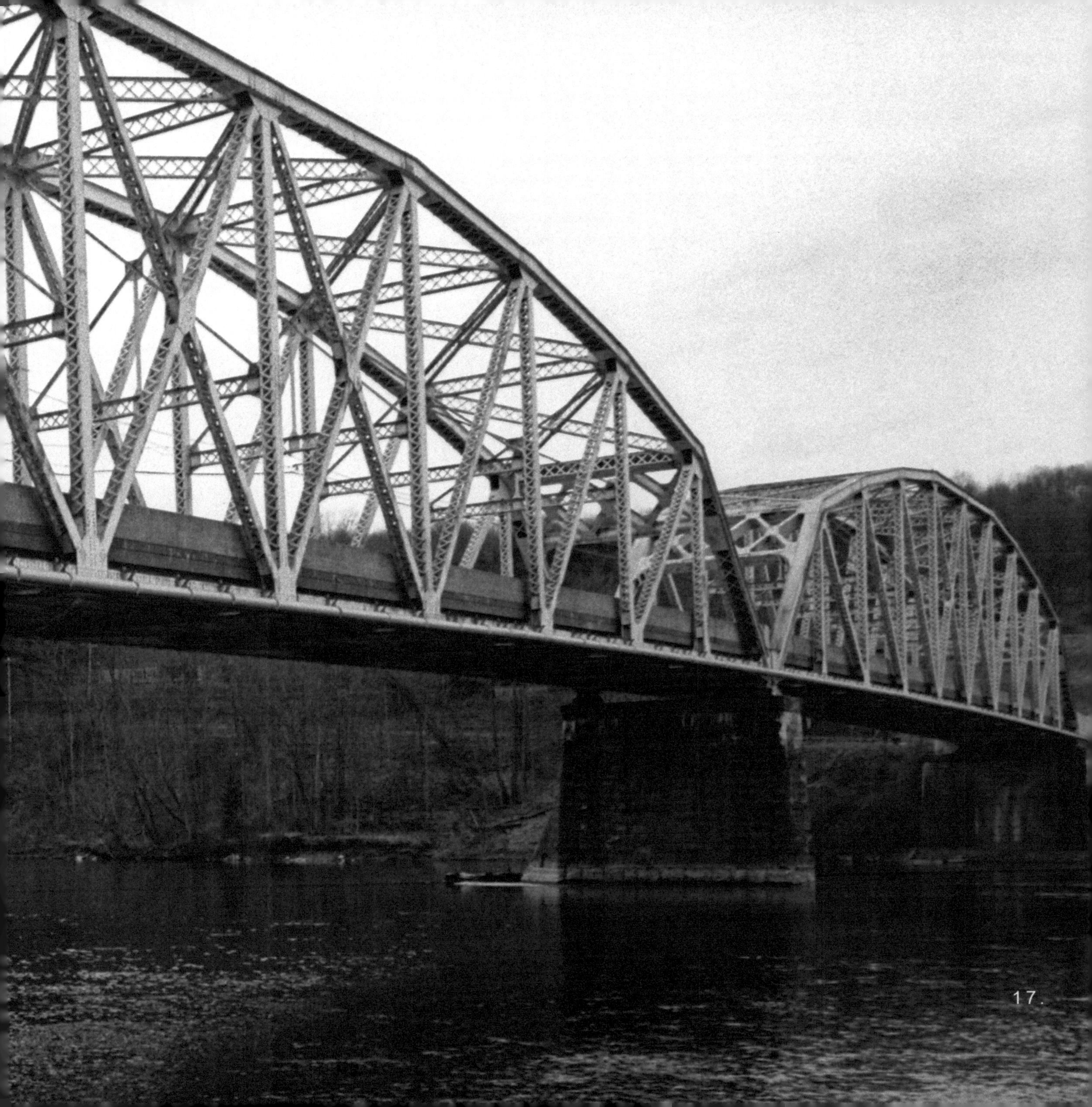
17.

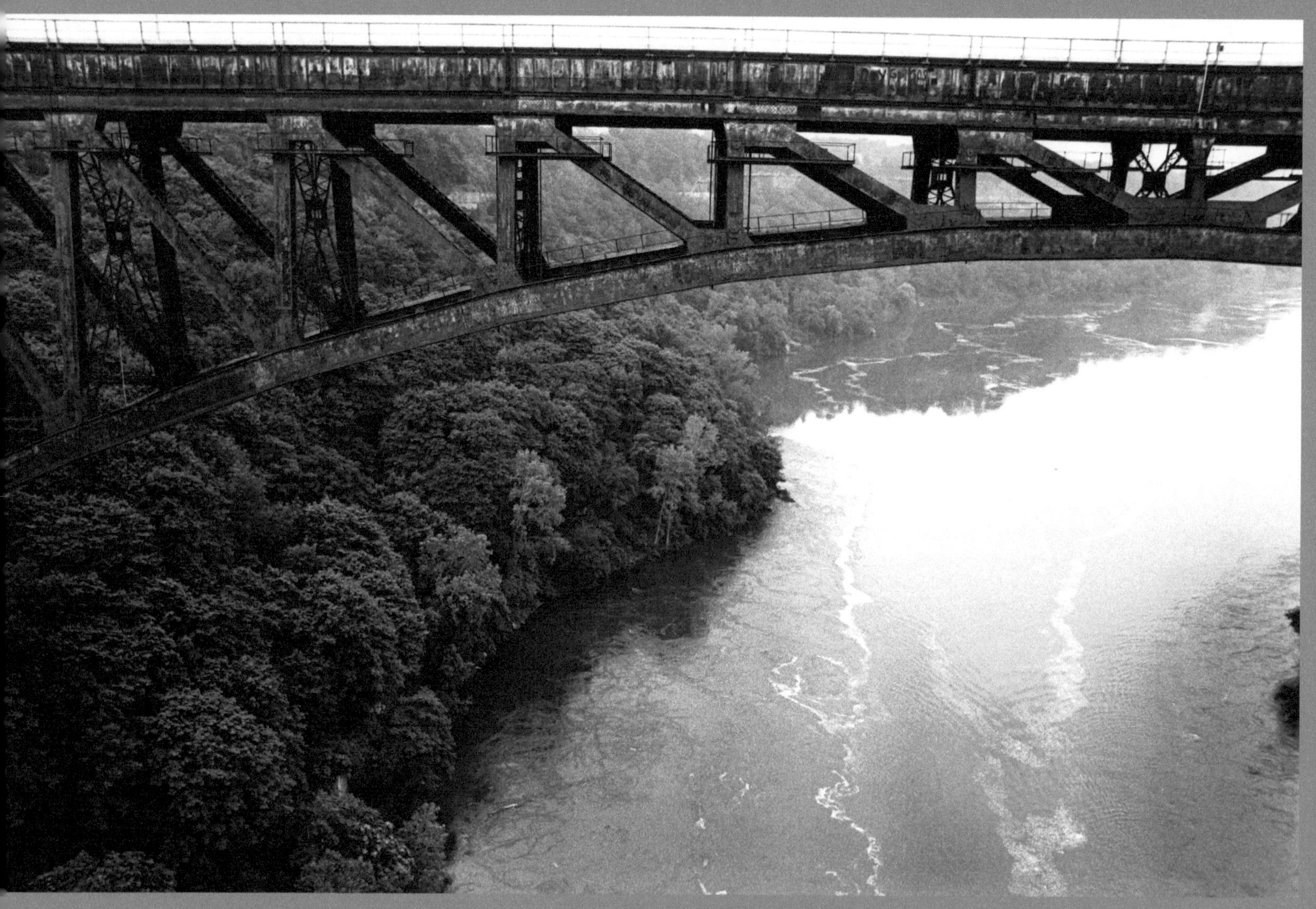

00-2872-22

If you find yourself in Upstate New York and have the misfortune of eating a bad egg and wish to clear your upper gastrointestinal system, look no further than a pair of Niagara bridges to facilitate a vomitorium; stepping out on the highway bridge and looking underneath the sister railroad bridge will do the trick.

Enormous arched bridges spanning deep and rugged gorges are often so placed, making it difficult to find an appropriate field of view. I snapped this shot with my 10-year-old daughter at my side and a worried mother watching from the safety of Canadian terra firma. We are looking at the Whirlpool Rapids Railroad Bridge from a vantage point on the Whirlpool Rapids Highway Bridge. Last check, there have been on-again/off-again discussions of demolishing the railroad bridge. Let's hope it ain't so.

Pages 20+21 show two views of the South Grand Island Bridge, actually bridge(s), two identical spans that cross the Niagara River. Built decades apart, one was built in 1935 and the other in 1963, using the same plans and methods. I was there 23 years ago, and I'm not sure which bridge is which in my photos. The larger view shows a span with peeling and cracking paint; the close-up is newly painted metal. This indicates I have shots of both spans, one under incomplete maintenance. No matter; they are beautiful steel arch bridges with suspended decks and no plans circulating to replace them.

Our next stop takes us to Maryland and the Chesapeake waters as they narrow into the mouth of the Susquehanna River. Volume 2 spends a lot of time on the Susquehanna; it's a large and twisting river with lots of bridges to discuss and is close to home because we live in the hills of Central PA overlooking the Susquehanna.

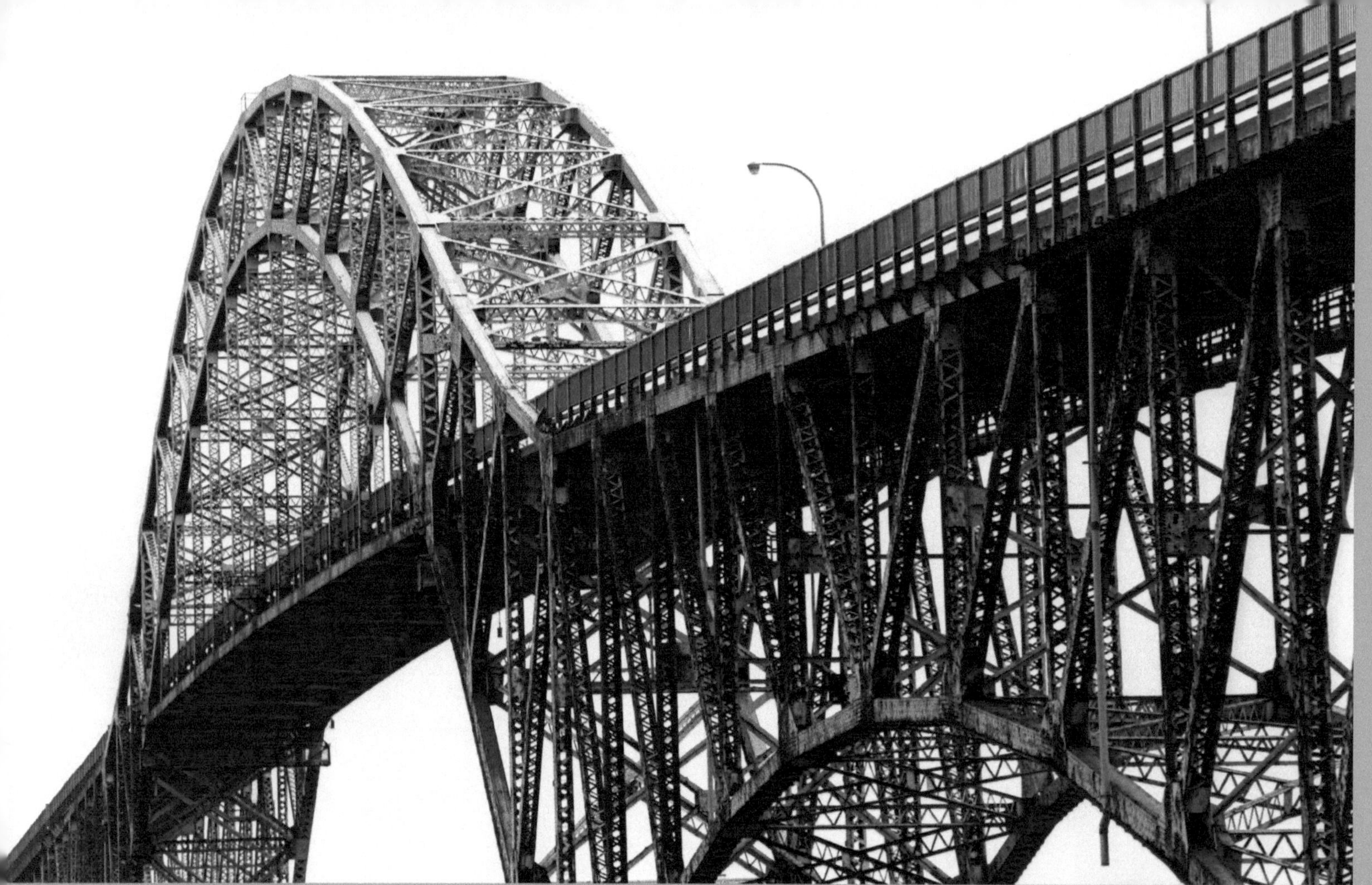

00-2899-01

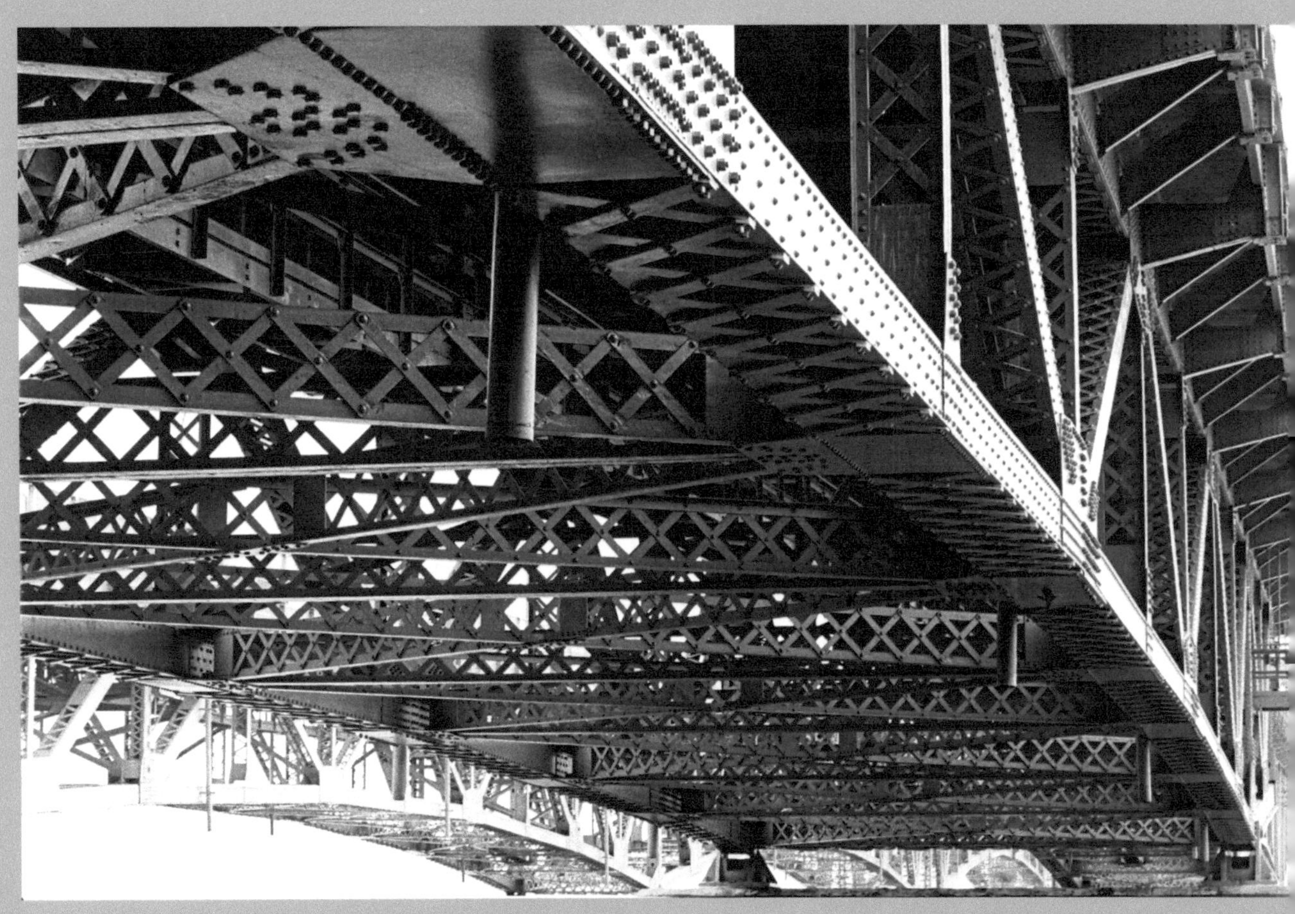

00-2877-18

The Francis Scott Key Bridge, pictured right, is an *arch-shaped continuous* through truss bridge and ranks 3rd in truss length worldwide. It crosses Baltimore's Outer Harbor as part of a beltway route. It has a conspicuous presence and is familiar to my travel history of going back and forth between Philadelphia and Washington, D.C., throughout my time as a professional sculptor. I include it as the southern-most marker of my Mid-Atlantic explorations.

In ***Bridges*** Volume 1, I spill a lot of ink on the *continuous* truss bridge design. I won't repeat it here except to remind readers that "continuous" refers to how the bridge forces are shared without breaks along its entire length. In the case of the Francis Scott Key Bridge, it's one giant arch-shaped truss. As we begin our way up the Susquehanna River, we will find many spectacular *simple truss* spans in counter-distinction to the *continuous truss*. We will revisit this topic in the following pages.

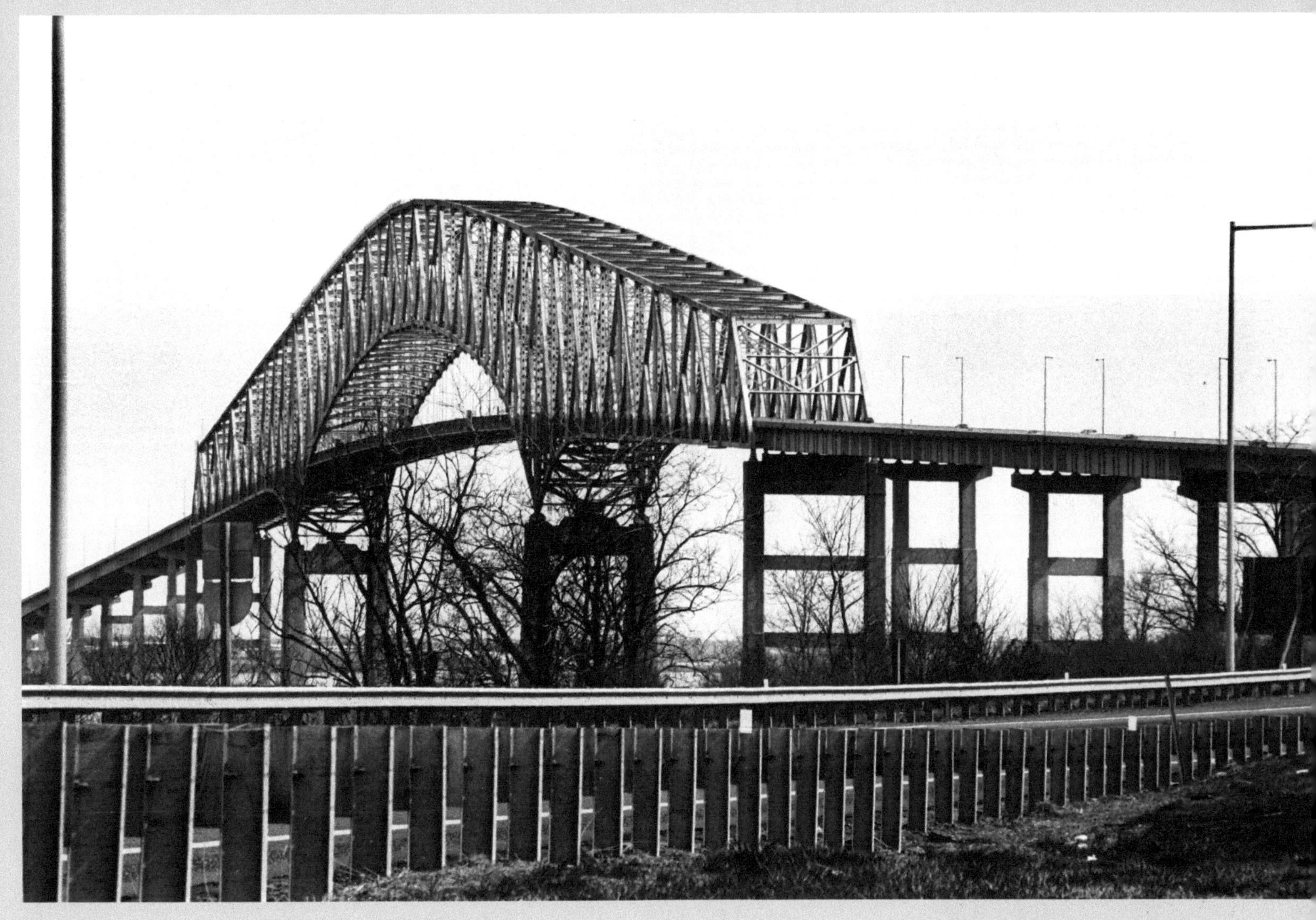

02-6962-15

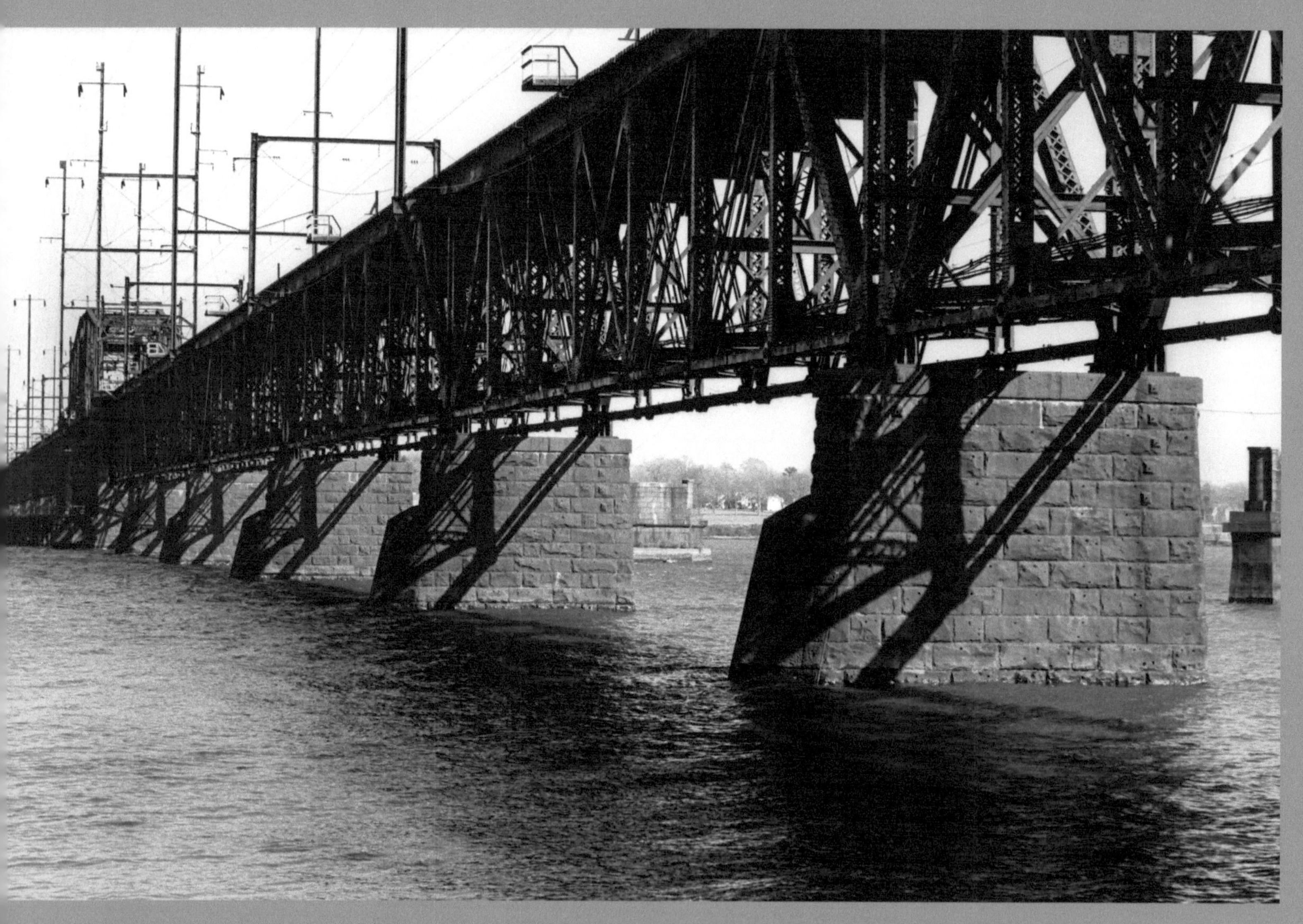

01-3758-02

01-6645-28 Overleaf

24.

Page 24 shows us the Amtrak Bridge at Havre de Grace, Maryland. About 100 trains running at 90 mph cross the span each weekday. It is located on the ending waters of the Susquehanna at a place used as a crossing for over 300 years, starting as a ferry boat site in 1695. Since then, bridges have come and gone, but the need to cross the water hasn't changed.

Pages 26+27 have a panoramic view with the Chesapeake Bay in the distance. A few yards past the bridge are the remains of the piers belonging to the previous span. The Amtrak Bridge was put into service in 1906, and plans are confirmed for its replacement, with construction to begin in 2023. I'm glad my pages hold a flame in memory of the old span.

Our next stop is a short distance upstream and continues the story of Havre de Grace's place of importance as a Susquehanna River crossing.

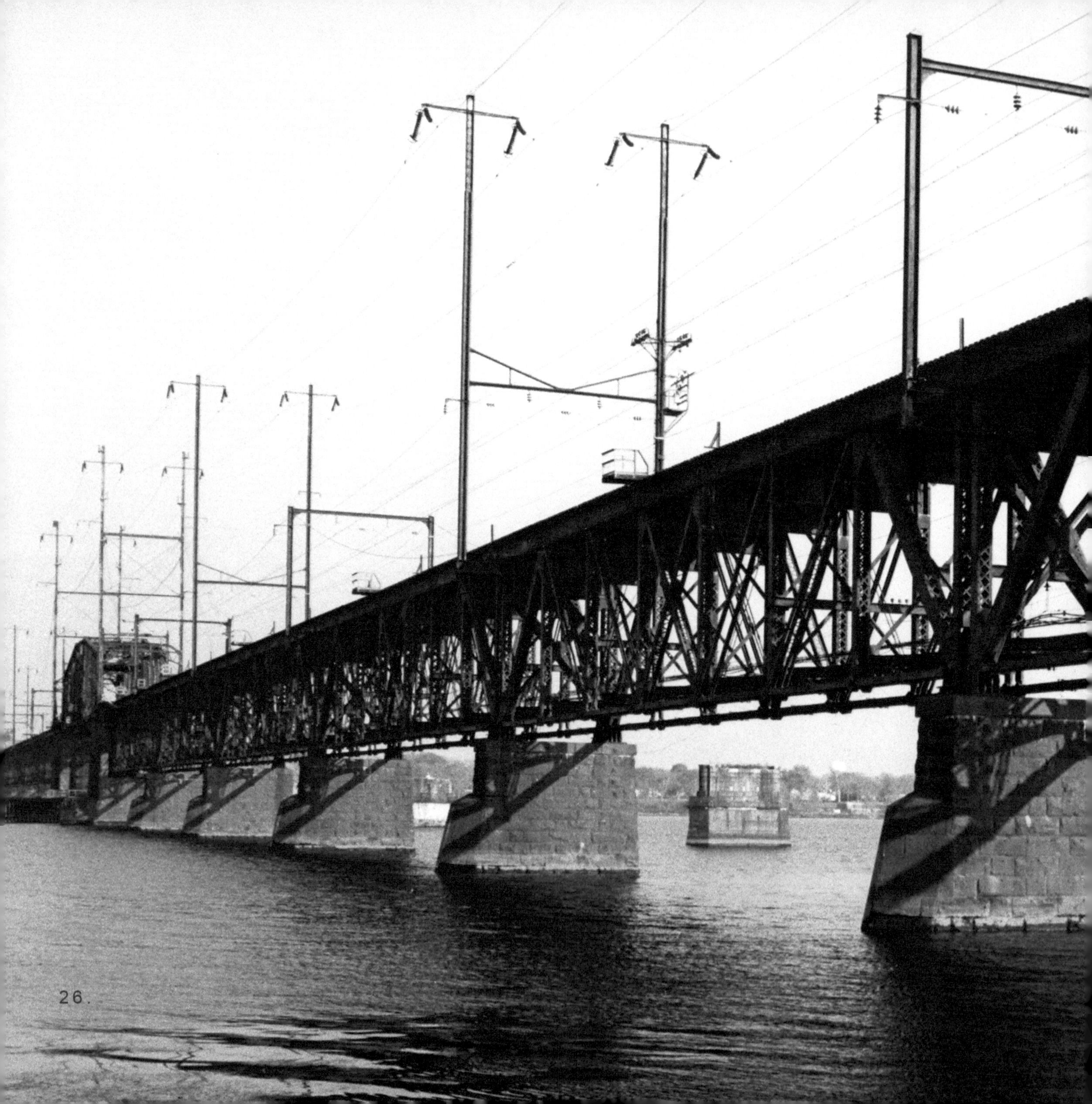

26.

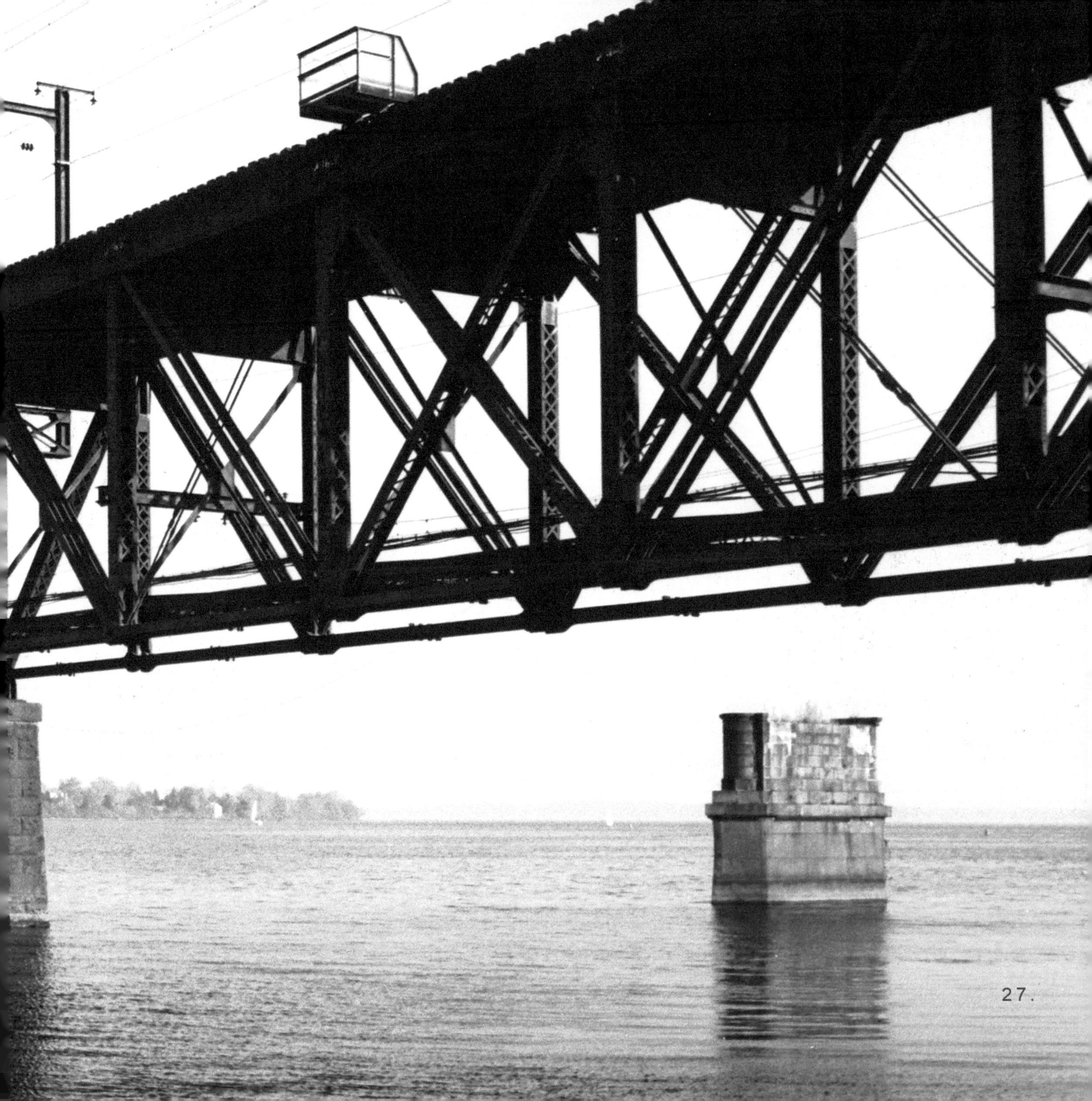

27.

The Havre de Grace Railroad Bridge is a *Baltimore* truss design, which is a reinforced *Pratt* truss. You may remember the Pratt configuration has the diagonals “V” toward the bottom/center of the truss. The Baltimore adds some metal onto those diagonals, confusing the geometry but strengthening the original Pratt design.

Pages 30+31 have a detailed view of the pier where the *deck* truss switches to a *through* truss. A deck is where the tracks run on top of the truss structure; a through truss is where the train runs under, or “through,” the truss. So-far/so-good. The point where the two types of trusses meet over the pier is a perfect example of *discontinuity*, where the bridge forces of tension and compression are not shared between trusses. Each truss is a self-standing smaller bridge placed end-to-end to make a longer span; no structural forces are passed over the piers to the adjacent truss.

All of this seems self-evident, and it is, but I make a big deal of it because I want to clarify the distinction between the “discontinuous” truss and the “continuous” truss. The discontinuous truss bridge has a series of short, simple trusses connected end-to-end to complete the span. Whenever there are breaks in the flow of the structural forces, it’s called *discontinuity*. The *continuous* truss has the bridge forces shared, without pause, over the piers and the bridge’s entire length.

I wanted the air cleared over this issue because we will visit lots of multiple-span *simple truss* bridges that are enormous as we travel up the waters of the Susquehanna River. The Susquehanna tends to be shallow and wide, making it a candidate for long rows of simple truss bridges on many piers planted in the river bottom.

Traveling a short distance upstream brings us to the Havre de Grace, US Route 40 Bridge. Pictured on pages 32+33, the engineering record calls it a *Wichert* truss, a rare design I had never encountered. The span is a continuous truss with a suspended roadway, like the Francis Scott Key Bridge we looked at on page 23.

This completes our Maryland stops as we continue northward up the Susquehanna and begin looking at the spans Pennsylvania has to offer, which are many.

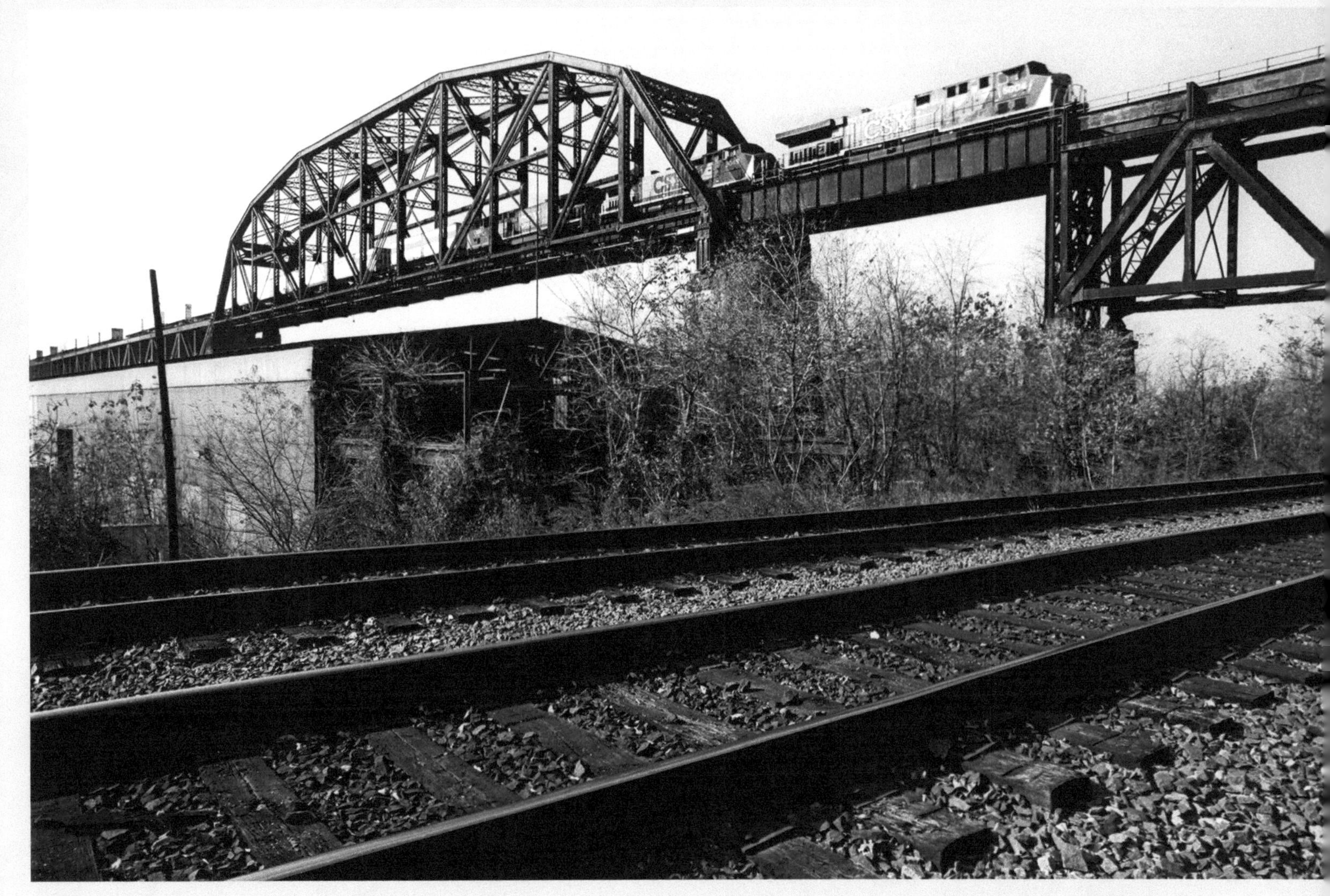


01-6646-24

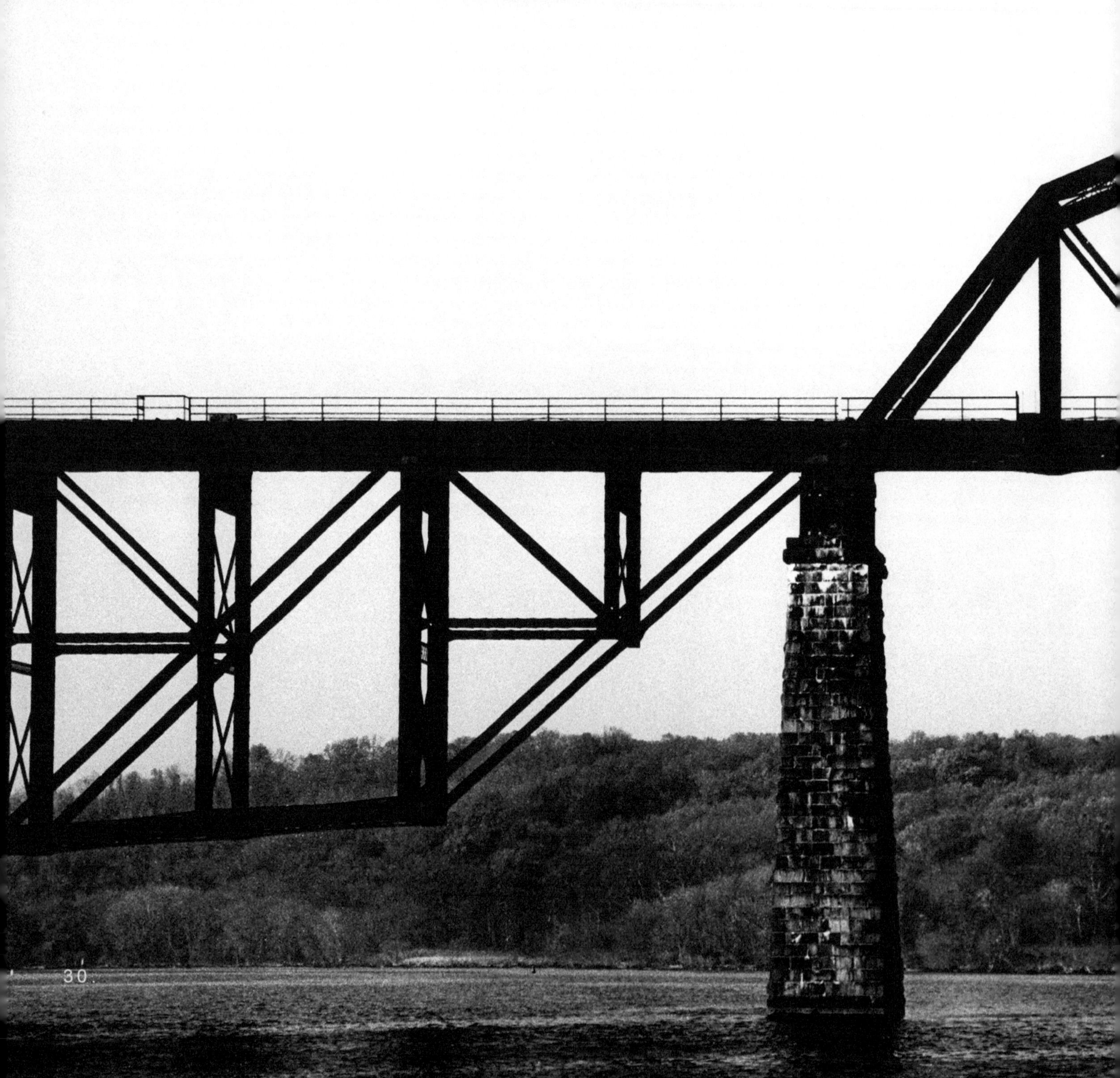

30.

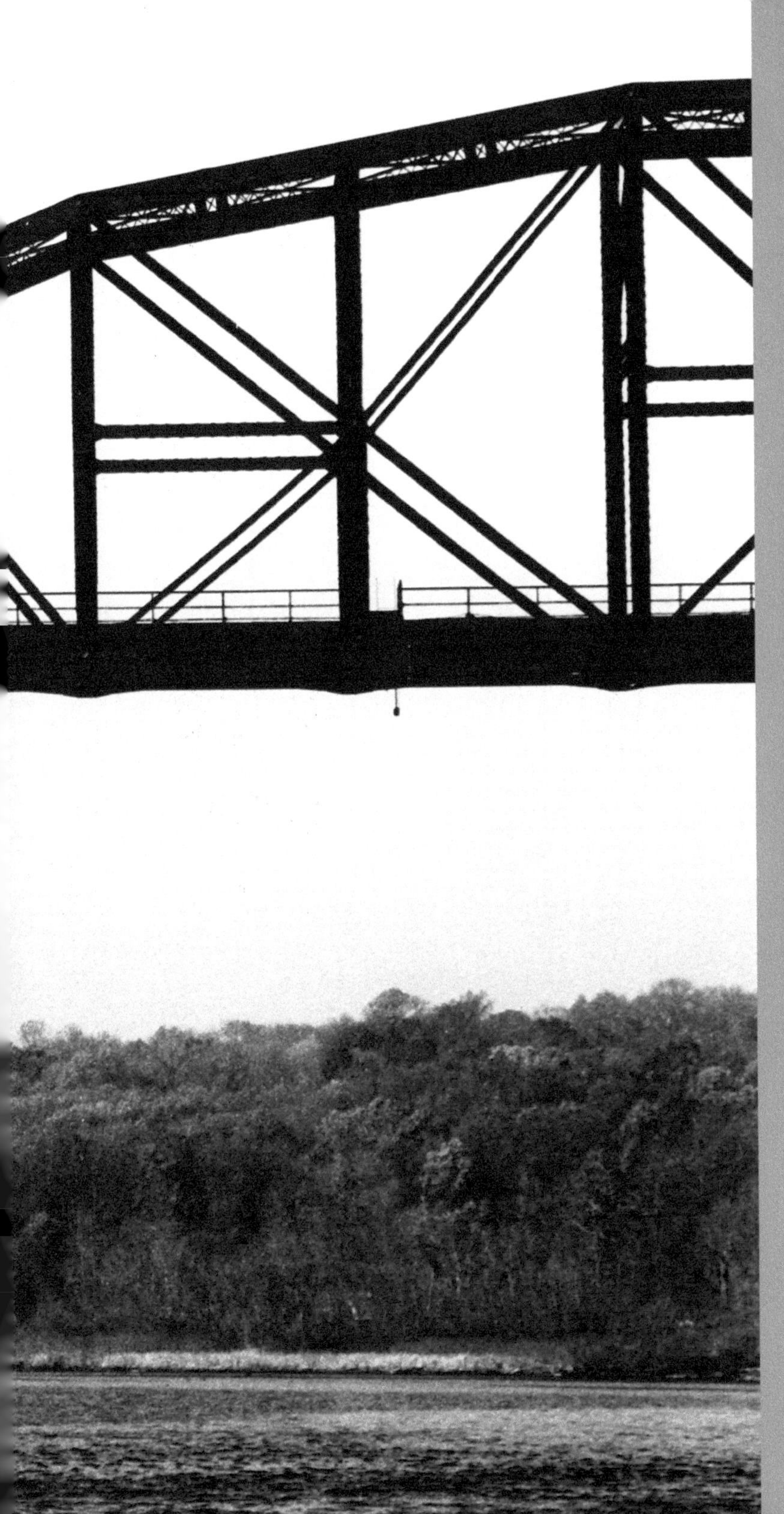

01-6647-33

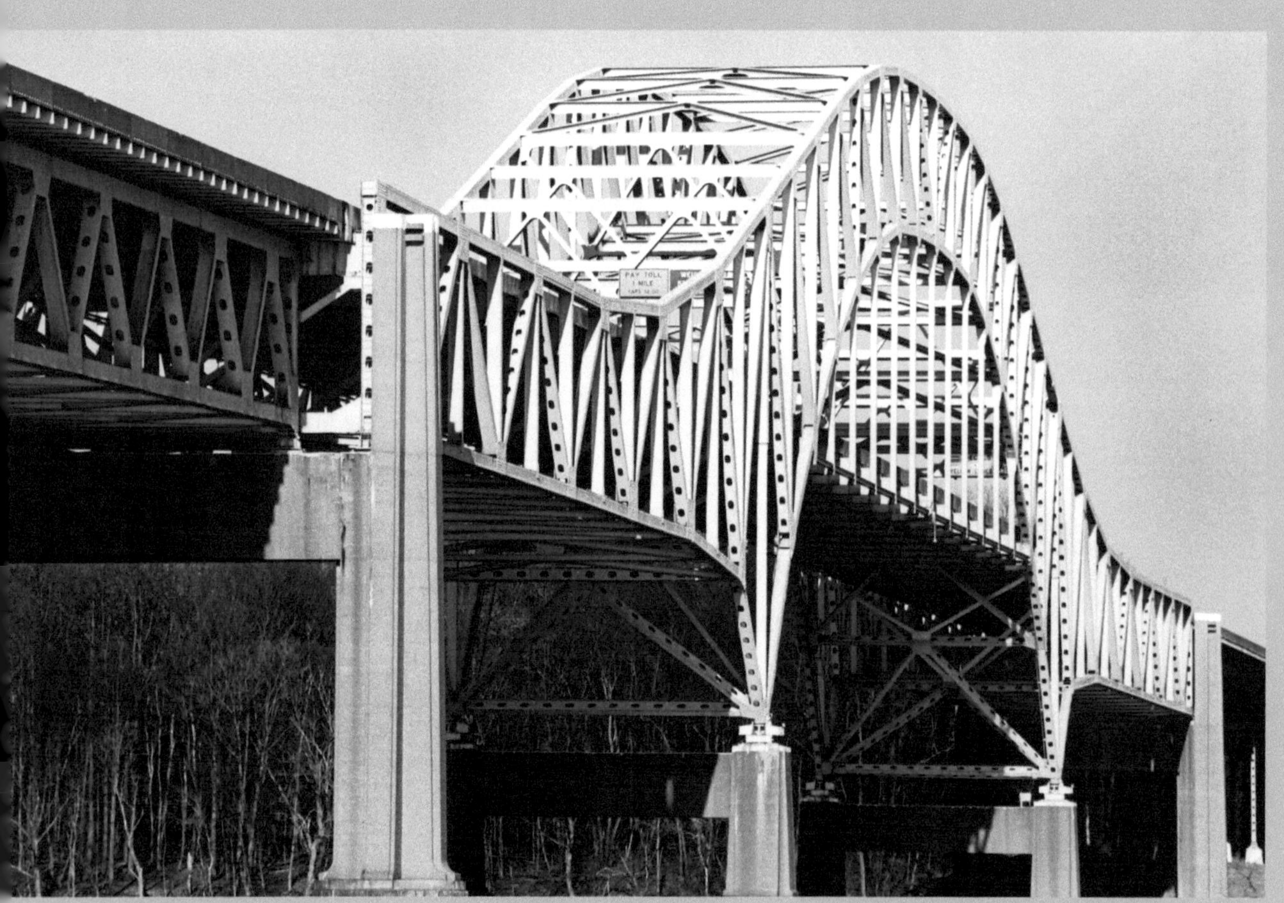


01-3757-27

32.

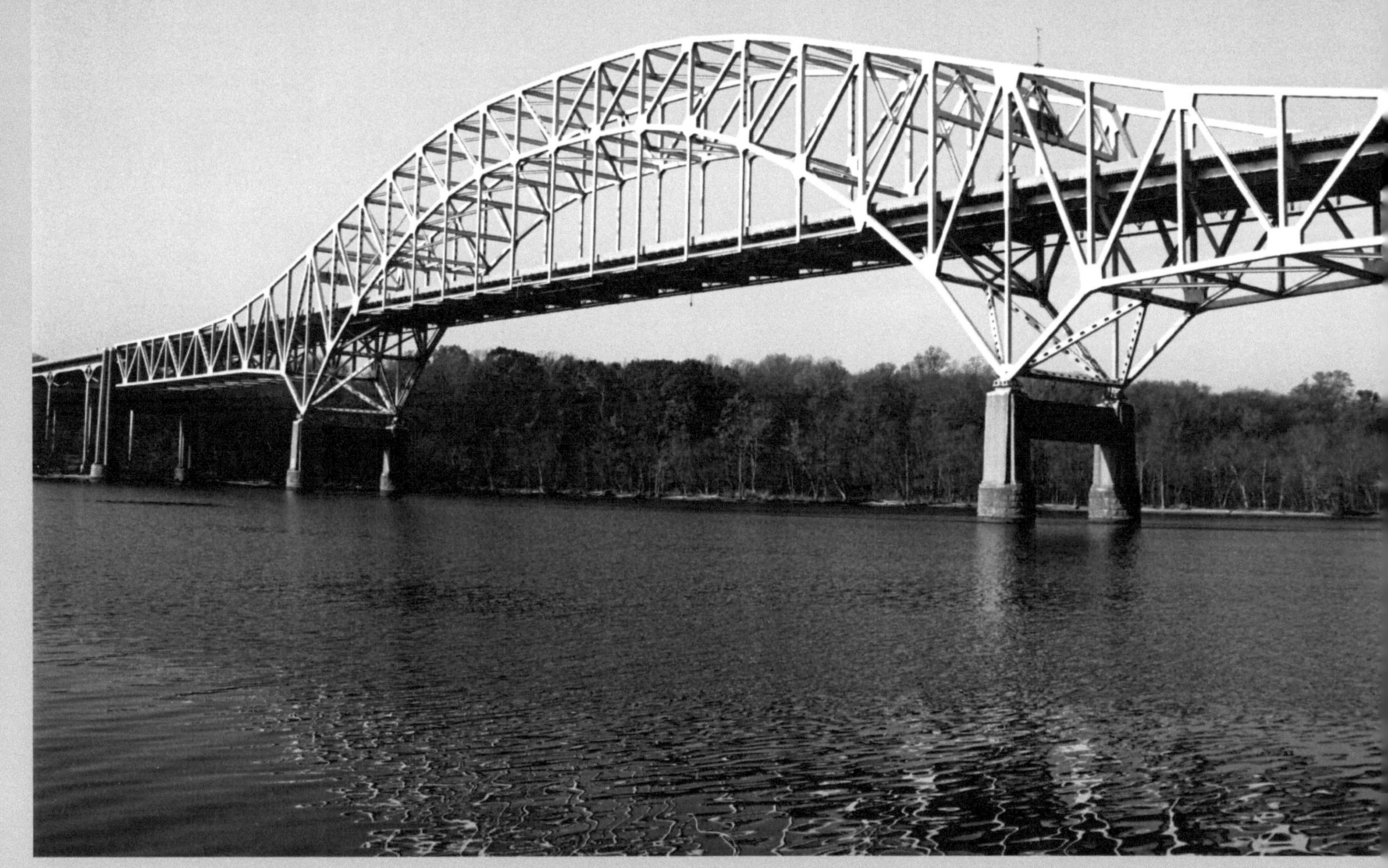

01-6644-23

Our first stop in Pennsylvania is the Selinsgrove Bridge, which carries trains over the Susquehanna River on 16 trusses of various designs, materials, and states of renovation. We will look at the longest part of the bridge, where nine truss sections span the river's main channel. The photo on page 35 is my "artsy" view, where I indulge the wooded banks and the textures of light on the ancient and sluggish Susquehanna currents. This river may be one of the oldest on the planet and looks that way.

In my Introduction essay to Volume 1 of ***Bridges***, I observe how bridges radically differ from the natural surroundings and are never mistaken for wild things; this remains true. However, equally natural, at least from the perspective of humanity, is the need and desire to cross rivers; it's as old as *Homo sapiens*. So, bridges have an almost primordial presence that transcends their difference with nature; confronting a vintage bridge in the wild seems naturally harmonious. I consciously want to capture this relationship whenever conditions permit, and the Selinsgrove Bridge is one of these subjects. Somehow, metal bridge geometry doesn't conflict with natural lines and substance. I will liberally indulge this visual profundity as we travel up and down the Susquehanna River.

Pages 36+37 have two more views. The Selinsgrove Bridge opened in 1890, with repairs and renovations carrying up to the present. All the trusses are constructed with *wrought iron* in the *Pratt* configuration, which has the diagonals angled toward the bottom/center, and the top chord is flat instead of curved. Wrought iron differs from steel, contradicting my ***Bridges*** trilogy's "steel bridge" focus. Expanding the books' sub-titles to include this exception seemed unnecessary; we're looking at ferrous bridges, and that's that. Most of the repairs performed on the original span were probably carried out with steel because metallurgy was progressing. Steel came into use in the second half of the 19th Century, and in Volume 3, we look at the first structure of any consequence built with the new material. It's called the Eads Bridge, spanning the Mississippi River at St. Louis, MO. It opened in 1874, beating the Eiffel Tower by 15 years.

On a personal note, my daughter did her undergraduate studies in Selinsgrove at Susquehanna University, so the bridge and the region along the river have sentimental value in my family's story. The tired water of the Susquehanna cut into the equally ancient Appalachian hills, making my bridge photos postcards in a memory scrapbook.

A few miles upriver takes us to a place on the Susquehanna, where it splits into a main and West Branch. We follow the West Branch and look at four more classic bridges of varying designs; three still stand, and one fell to dynamite and the wrecking ball. Follow me for the ride.

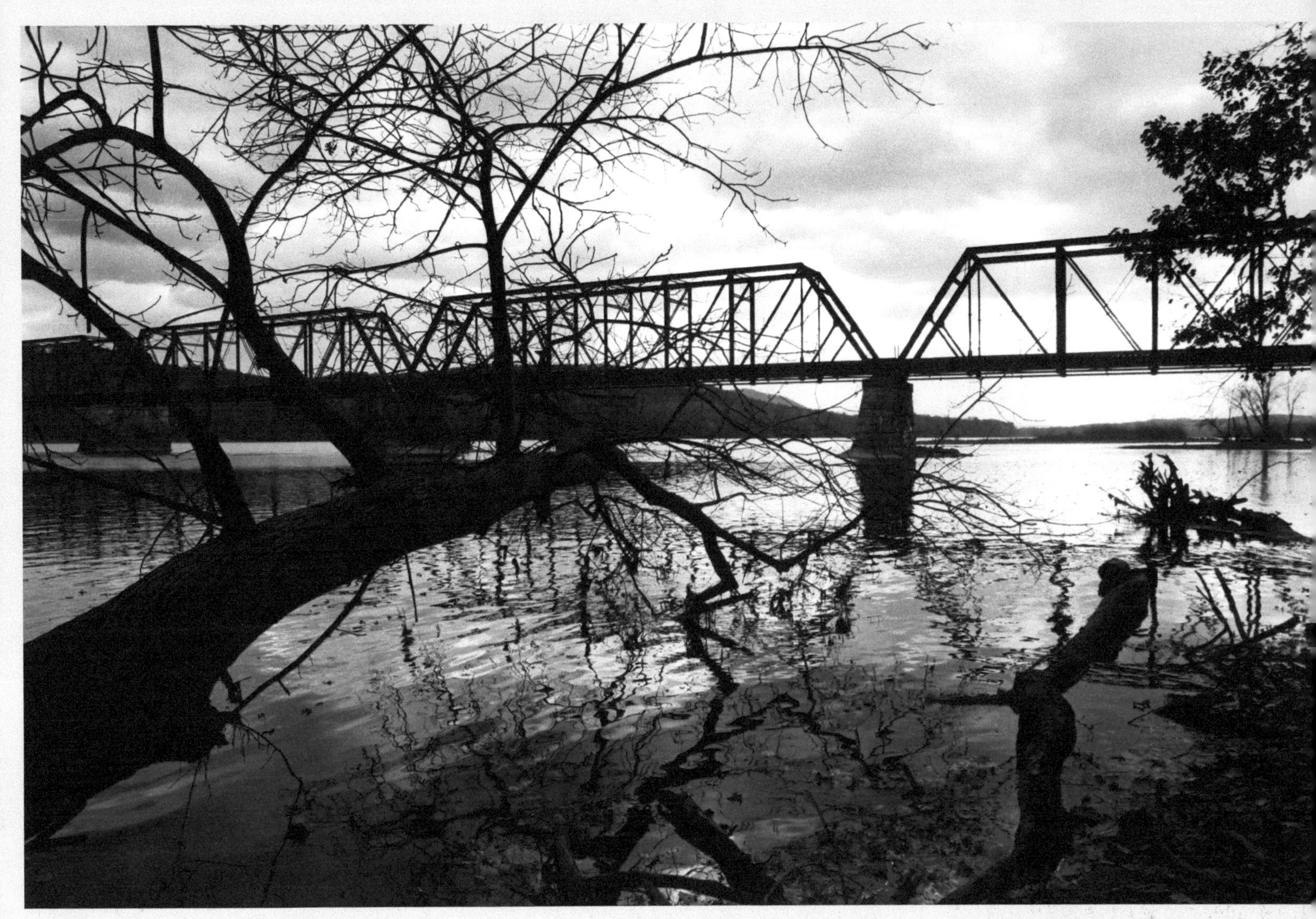

13-4811-25

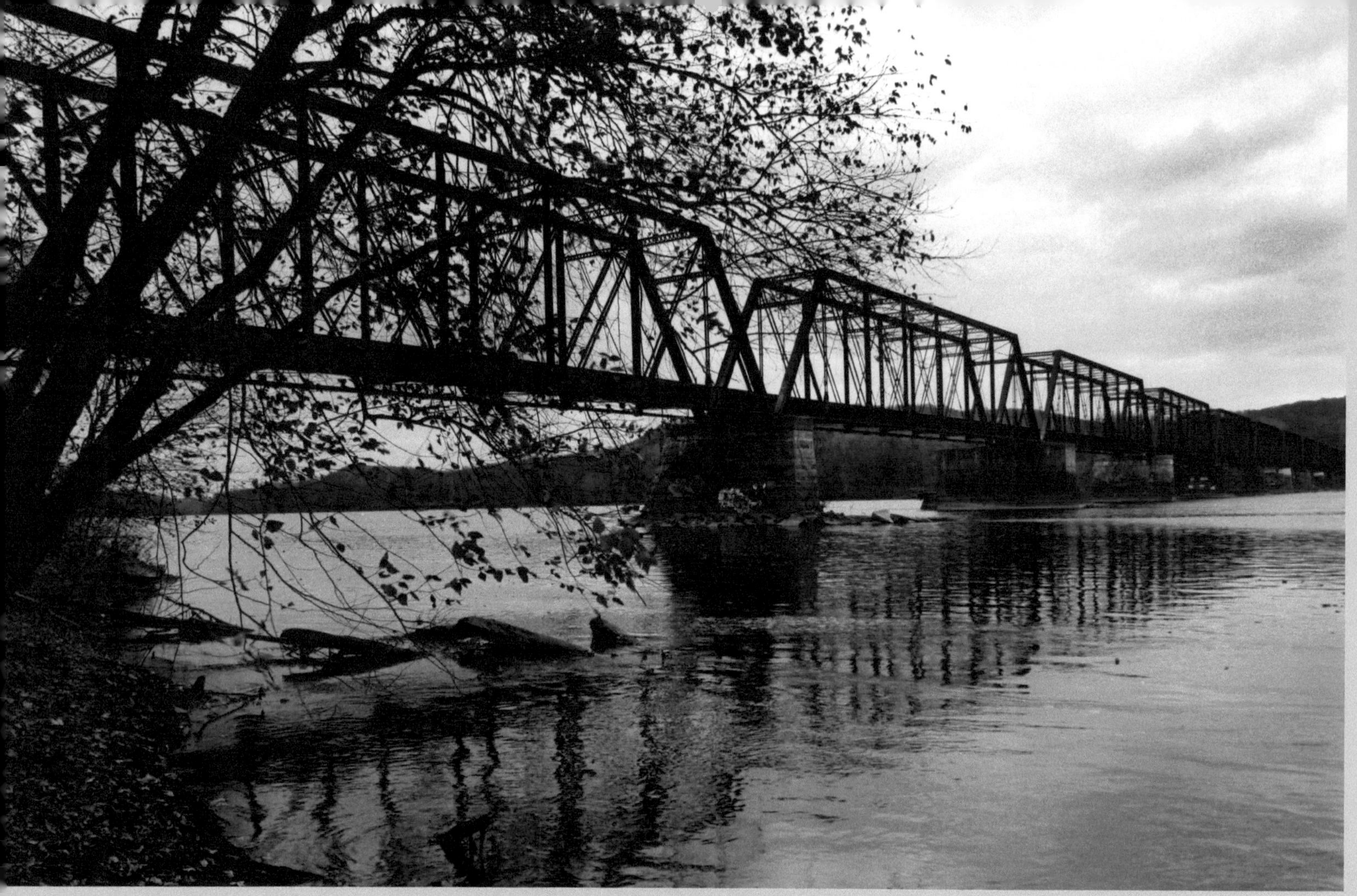

13-4812-03

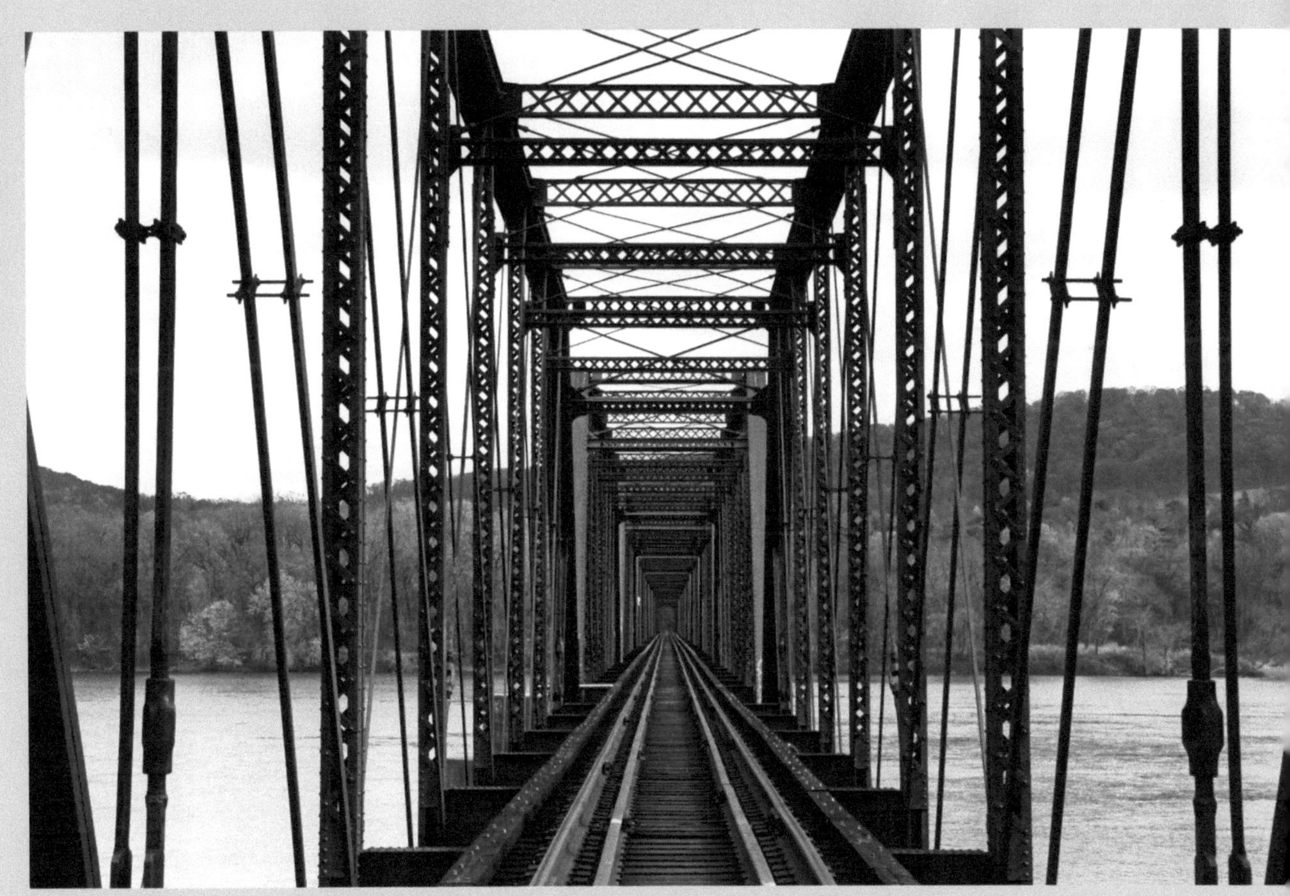

13-4814-08

The first stop on the West Branch is Lewisburg, a rather snazzy town uncharacteristic of Appalachia, where we sometimes go to pick up art supplies and have lunch. On page 39 is pictured the Lewisburg Pennsylvania Railroad Bridge, no longer in service and presently owned by the municipality to be converted for use as a rail trail. So far, the bridge sits unused. I'm fond of this view for the way the bridge shares the atmosphere with old-growth trees, and the highlights of snow define the subdeck metalwork and the stone-textured piers. However, the contemporary highway bridge in the distance messes up the otherwise antique look of the photo.

Overleaf 1 has another view of the Lewisburg Bridge, taken the same year but on a day without snow. The design is called a *Warren* truss, which I recognize for the prominent "W" shaped configuration and a flat top chord. This example has optional but equally prominent vertical members inside the "W"s.

Overleaf 2 has us upstream on the Susquehanna West Branch into Williamsport, where the Little League World Series is played yearly; I don't follow sports, so that's all I know. Williamsport is what my wife and I call "downtown." We've done numerous art events there; it's an excellent coffee shop destination, has many well-regarded restaurants, and features a supermarket with fantastic baked goods. It also had the Duboistown Bridge until 2012, when the geniuses in the roads department had it demolished.

I didn't see this one coming. One day, I traveled to Williamsport to get more photos of the bridge, couldn't find it, and thought I was going nuts. Nope. It was blown up in November. This solid bridge was suitable for continued service or retirement as a pedestrian and bicycle park; a well-used recreational path along the river levy makes the bridge a practical addition.

Pennsylvania used to be covered with truss bridge masterpieces, and they're quickly disappearing. The Duboistown Bridge is called a *camelback* truss, a rare design recognized by its five-part arched-shaped top chord; other types of arched-shaped truss configurations have seven or more. The internal geometry follows the same pattern as the Pratt truss. The Duboistown Bridge also retained much of its original stylistic details, making it essential as a museum relic worthy of preservation. None of this worked to save the thing.

To some readers, my attention to preservation is a call to resist infrastructure changes. Actually, I'm pro-modern. I'm an artist who once made a good living with a hyper-modern style of sculpture that required enough of an understanding of art to have an aesthetic sensibility that hungered to be satisfied. Modernity introduced many ideas, including the minimalist tendency that reduces things to transparent essentials in structure, function, and visual expression. This is no small gift to humanity and should be maintained. But we've confused modernism's aesthetics with a promise of an uncluttered future free of all ties to the past. Consequently, rootless souls create cacophonies of groundless myths believed to be history. Fear turns humanity into a reckless mob with nothing to lose after we've burned the bridges from whence we came.

The mixed metaphor is intentional. Steel bridges are necessarily built to last and are an accessible human resource to preserve as a public record of how modernism created a new aesthetic. Societal amnesia is the outcome of not doing so and can have catastrophic consequences.

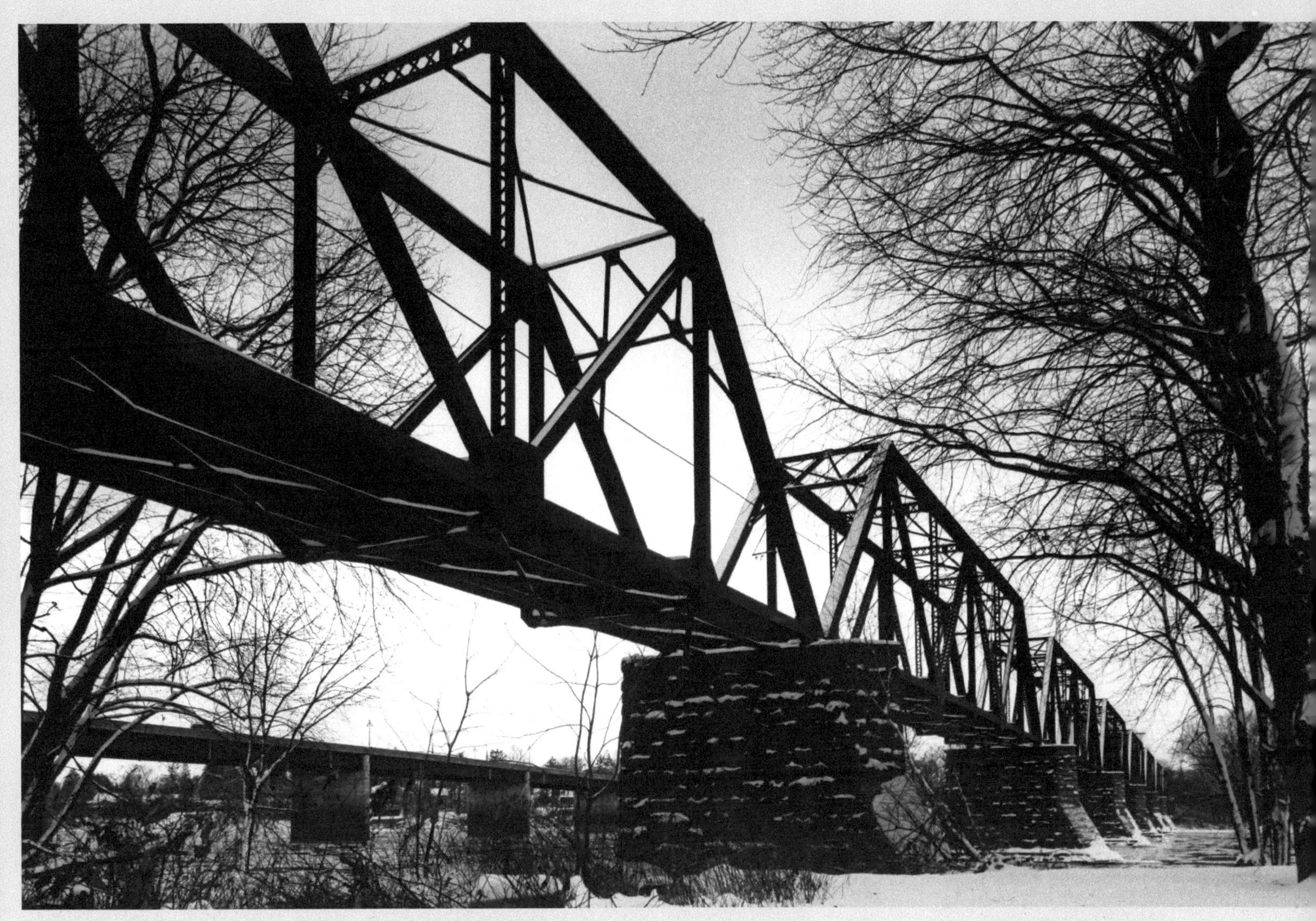

13-4826-13

Overleaf 1 13-4817-24

Overleaf 2 02-7328-12

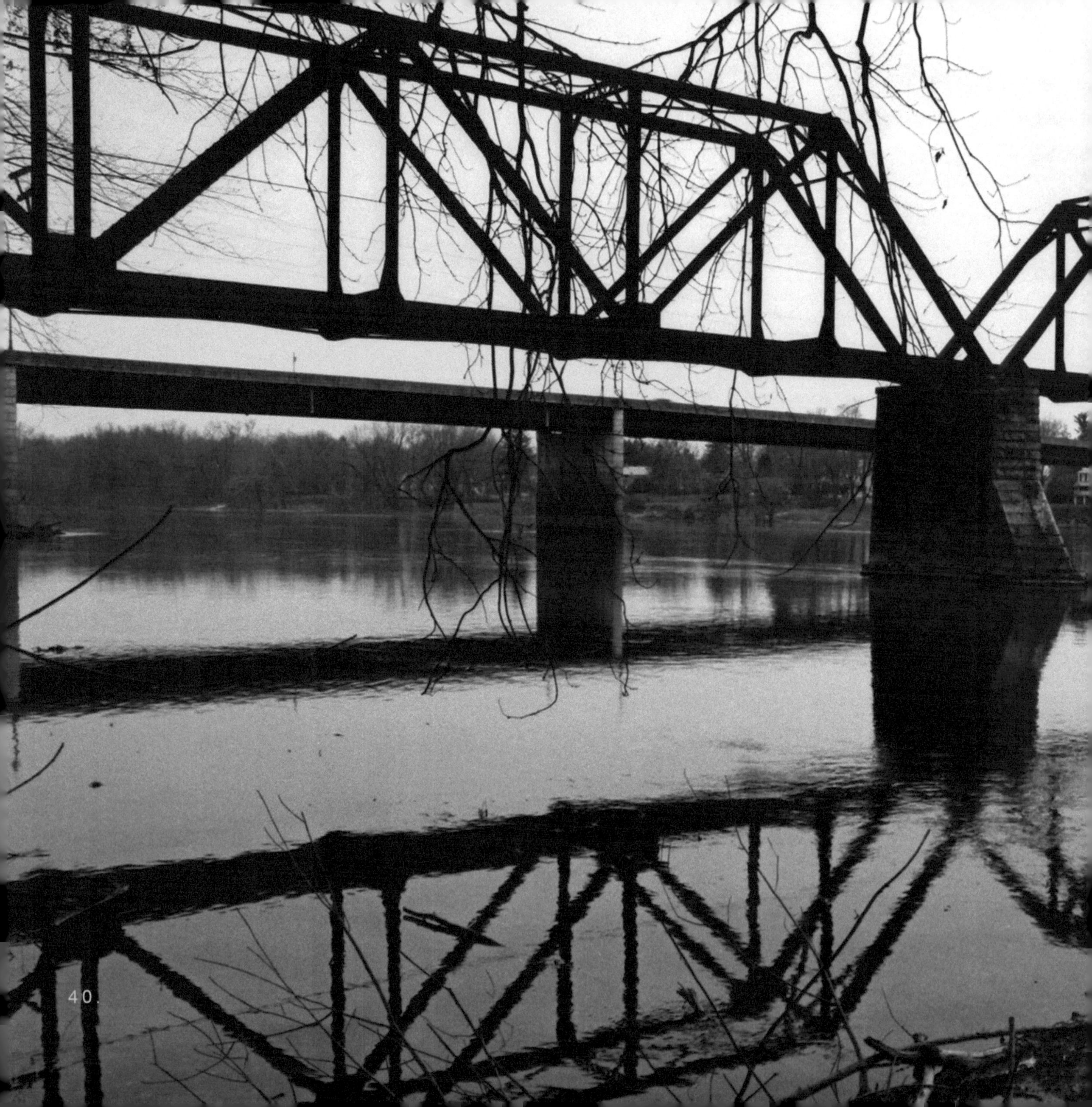

40.

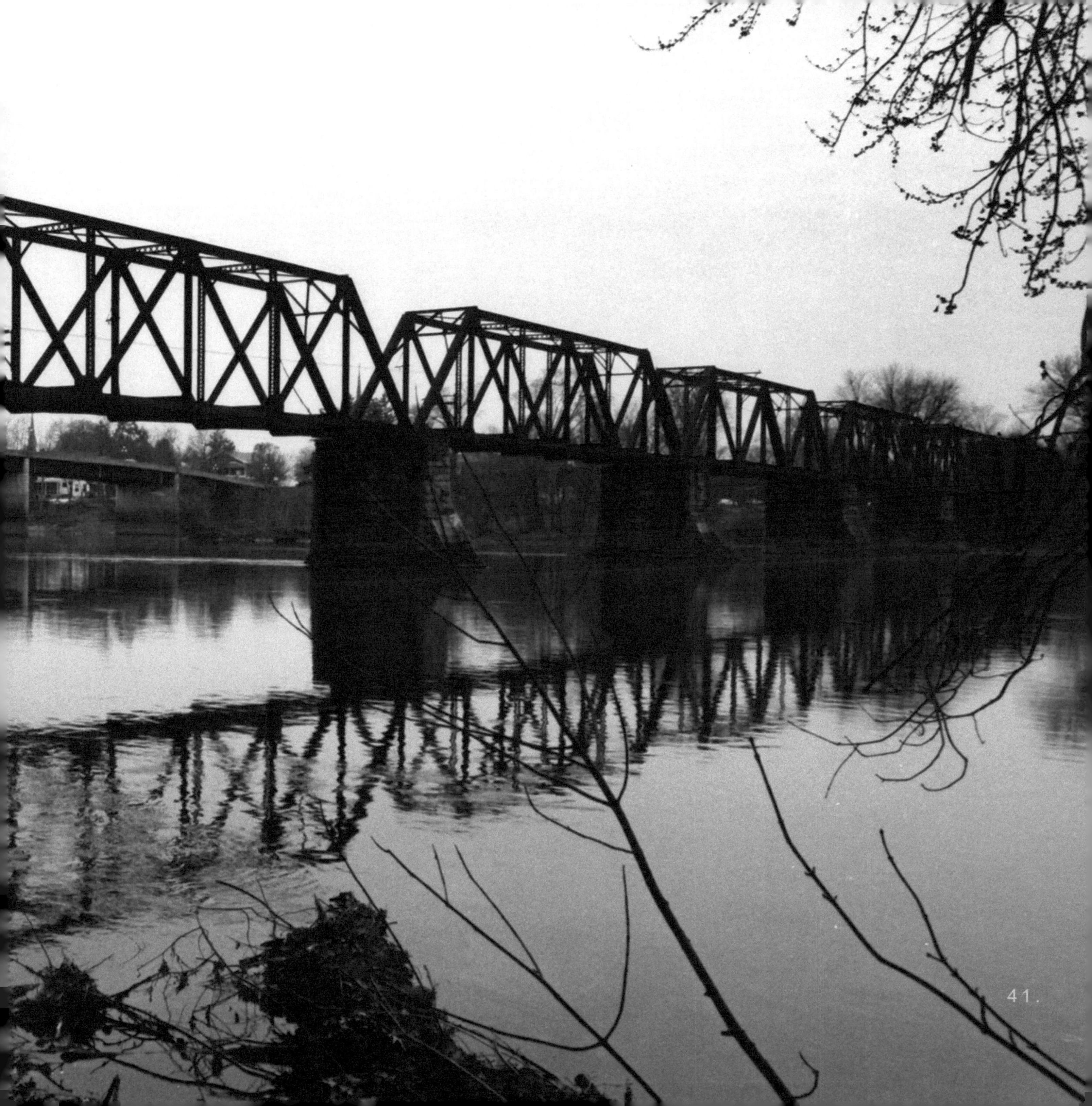

41.

42.

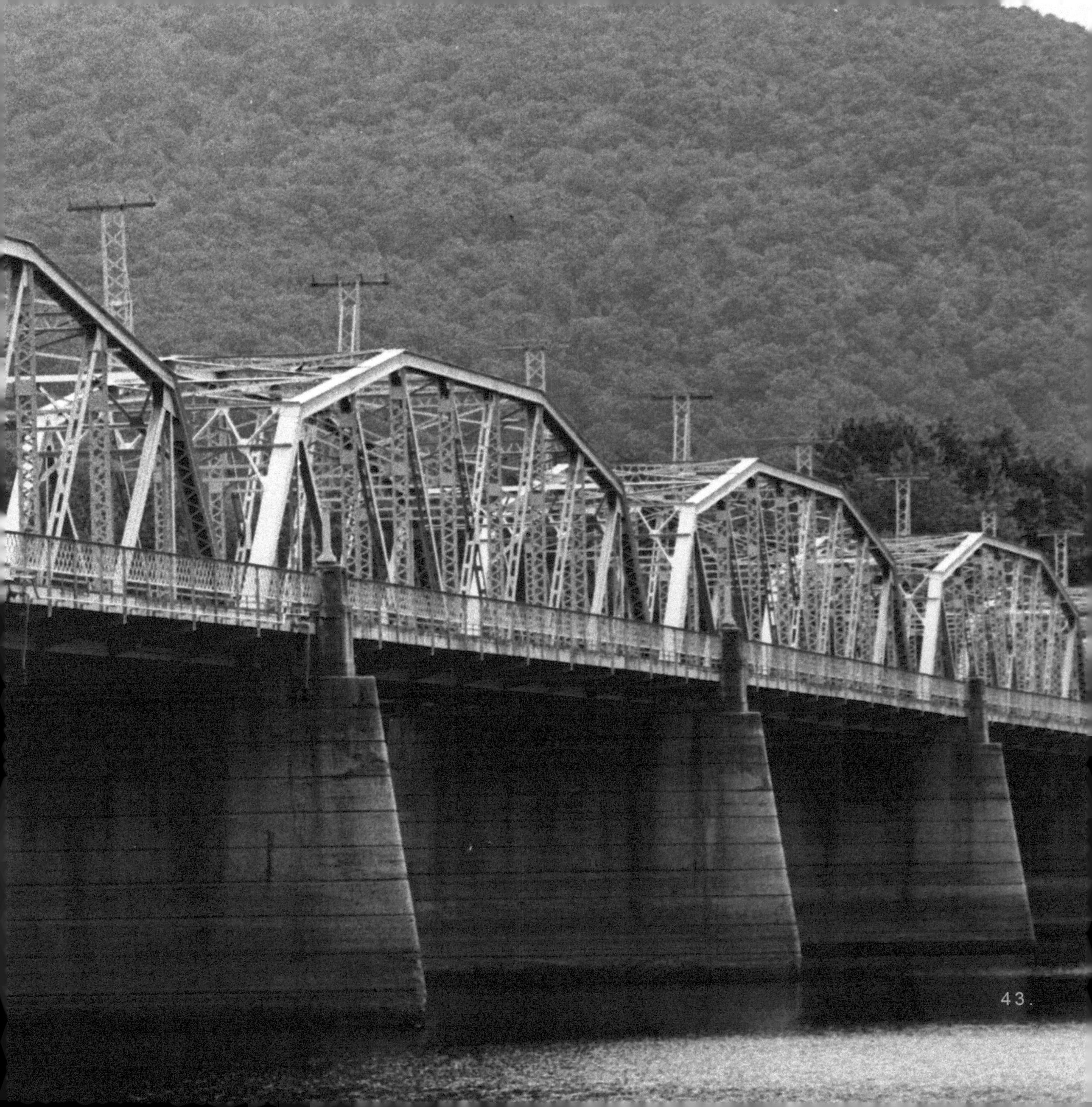

43.

Pages 45, 46, and 47 picture the Susquehanna River half frozen. A beautiful antique railroad bridge shares the stage with reflections from ice and water pools. These are some of my favorite photos, and they match the melancholy and introspection that consumed me during this period of my life. Here's my story.

In 2010, I woke up one day and found myself being trained as a substitute teacher for service in our region's public schools and juvenile prison facilities. The art markets had tanked, taking our pecuniary circumstances with it, forcing me to look for work. Yes, a real job, damn it, and the experience had more than a little to teach me about myself and the fragility of an artist's life. Luckily, I liked working in the prisons and probably got the better end of the deal in the long run; I learned more from the troubled kids than the other way around. I was repeatedly called upon to teach art, especially drawing, and prisons are places where the company has much to express in creative catharsis. I took up drawing after my experience and now make a living in my new media.

On the other hand, subbing in regular public schools felt like returning to a crime scene. Revisiting the noise and smells of institutional learning caused soul-searching as I experienced school in the front of the classroom instead of daydreaming in the back. Growing up, I hated school. On more than one occasion, teachers contacted my mother, wondering if I'm hard-of-hearing or exhibiting something arising from other issues. A life of artmaking is a natural consequence of my predicament, with only God to thank for handing me enough talent to make it work as well as it has, which is far from stellar, but I've made it this far.

Now, back to the bridge: Called the Lycoming Valley Railroad Bridge, this is a seven-span *Warren* through truss. Warren trusses have "W" shaped diagonals with optional vertical members inside the "W"s. (Most of the Warren trusses I discuss in this volume have the vertical members present.)

Next, we follow the West Branch to our last stop, the Jersey Shore Bridge, also called the Pine Creek Bridge, an elegant single-span lenticular truss on a lonely corner of the Pine Creek tributary to the larger river. Then we jump to New York State, where we pick up the main branch of the Susquehanna close to the headwaters and look at a few more lenticular truss bridges. I began discussing this type of truss in the early pages of Volume 1 with the Smithfield Street Bridge in Pittsburgh. The following bridges are smaller and of reduced stature, but equally beautiful.

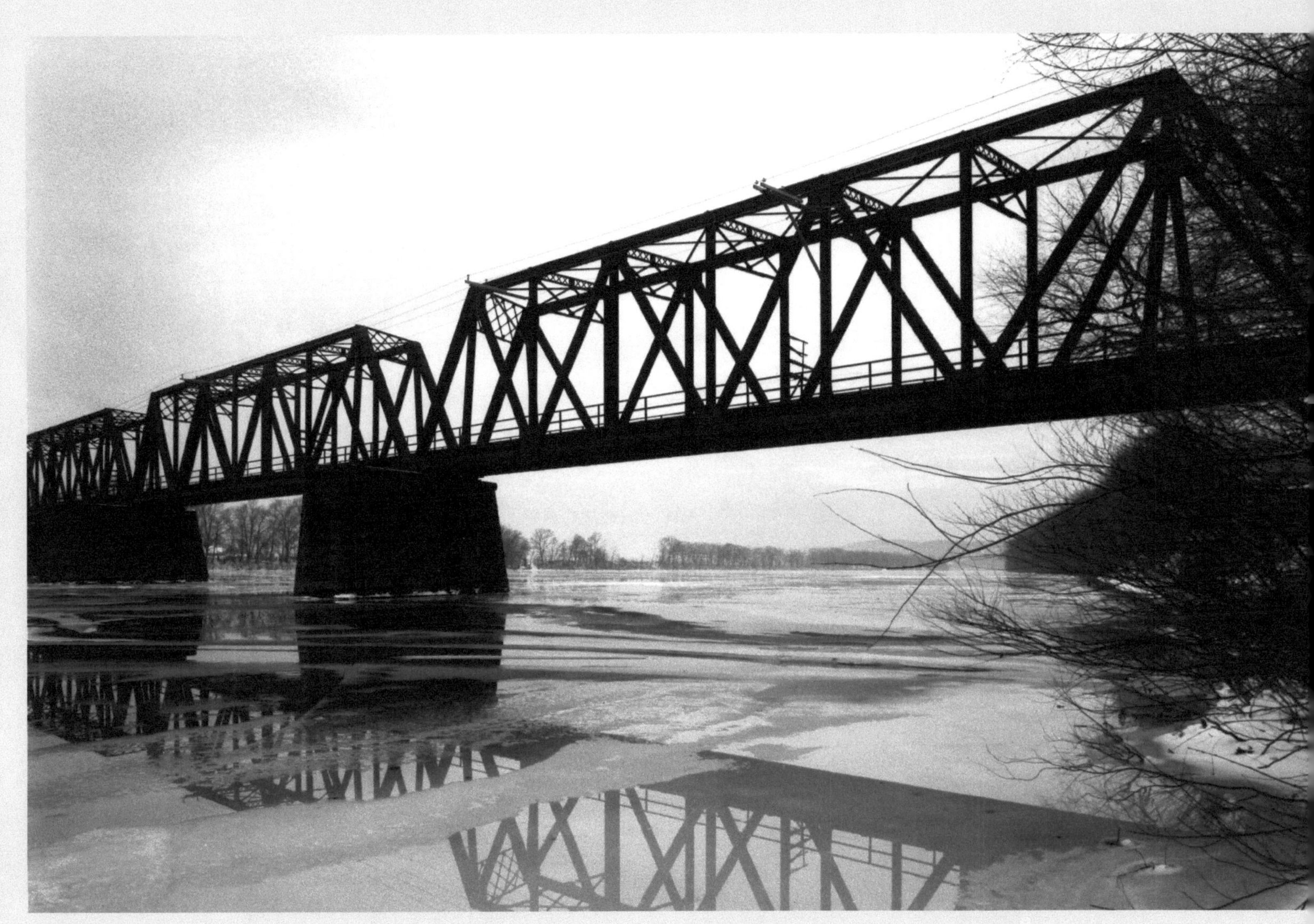

14-4828-11
Overleaf 14-4828-27

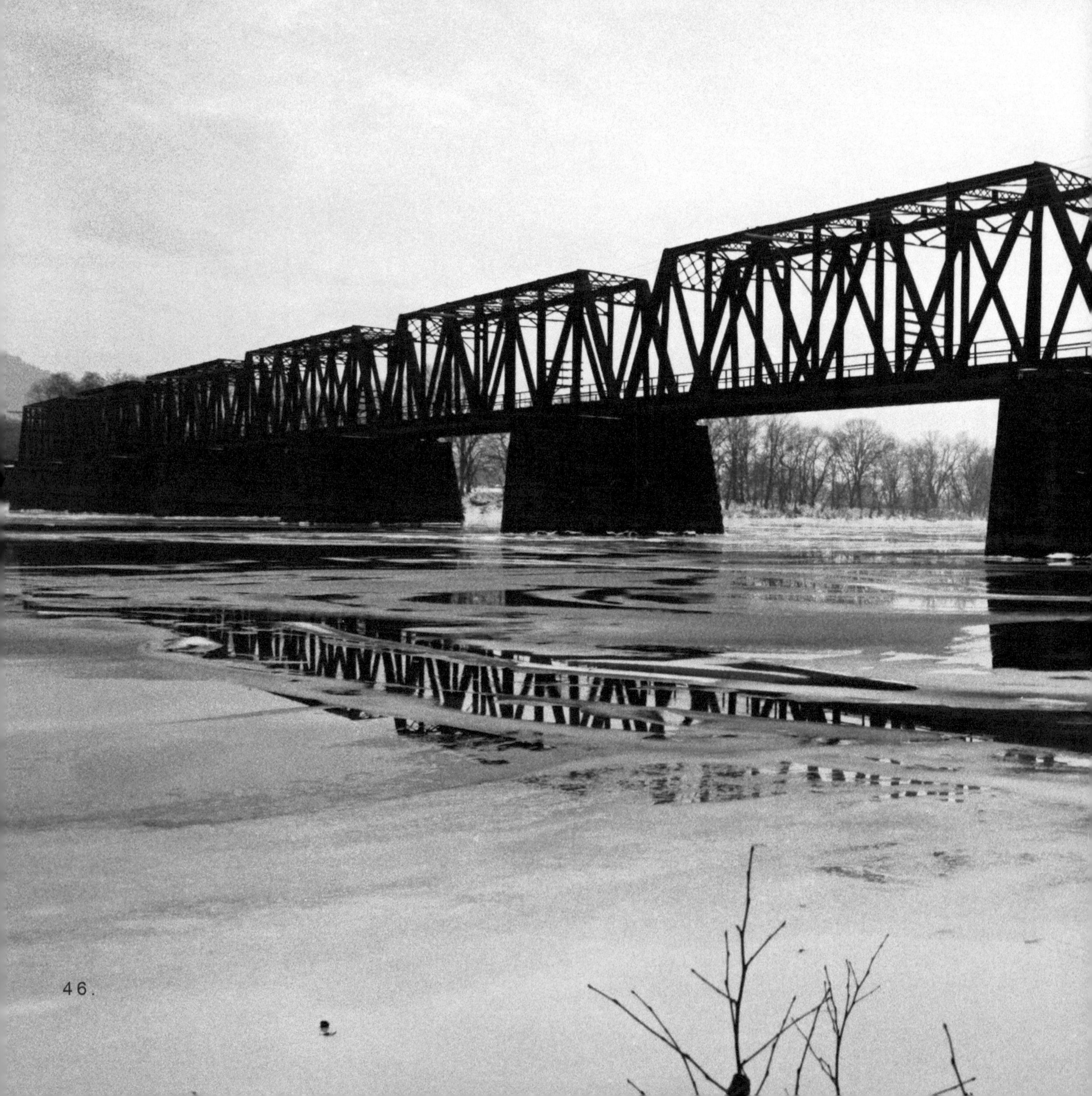

46.

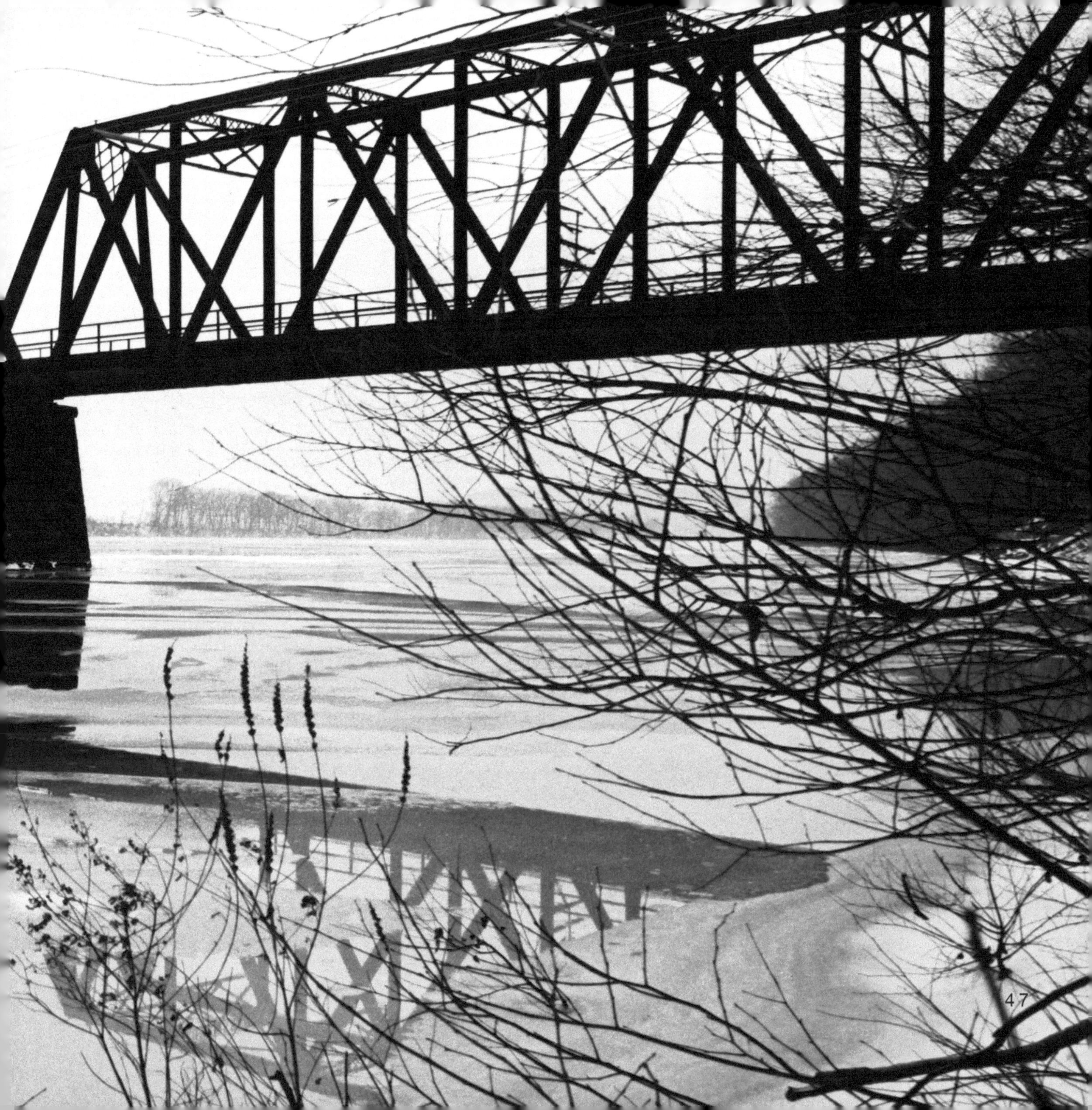

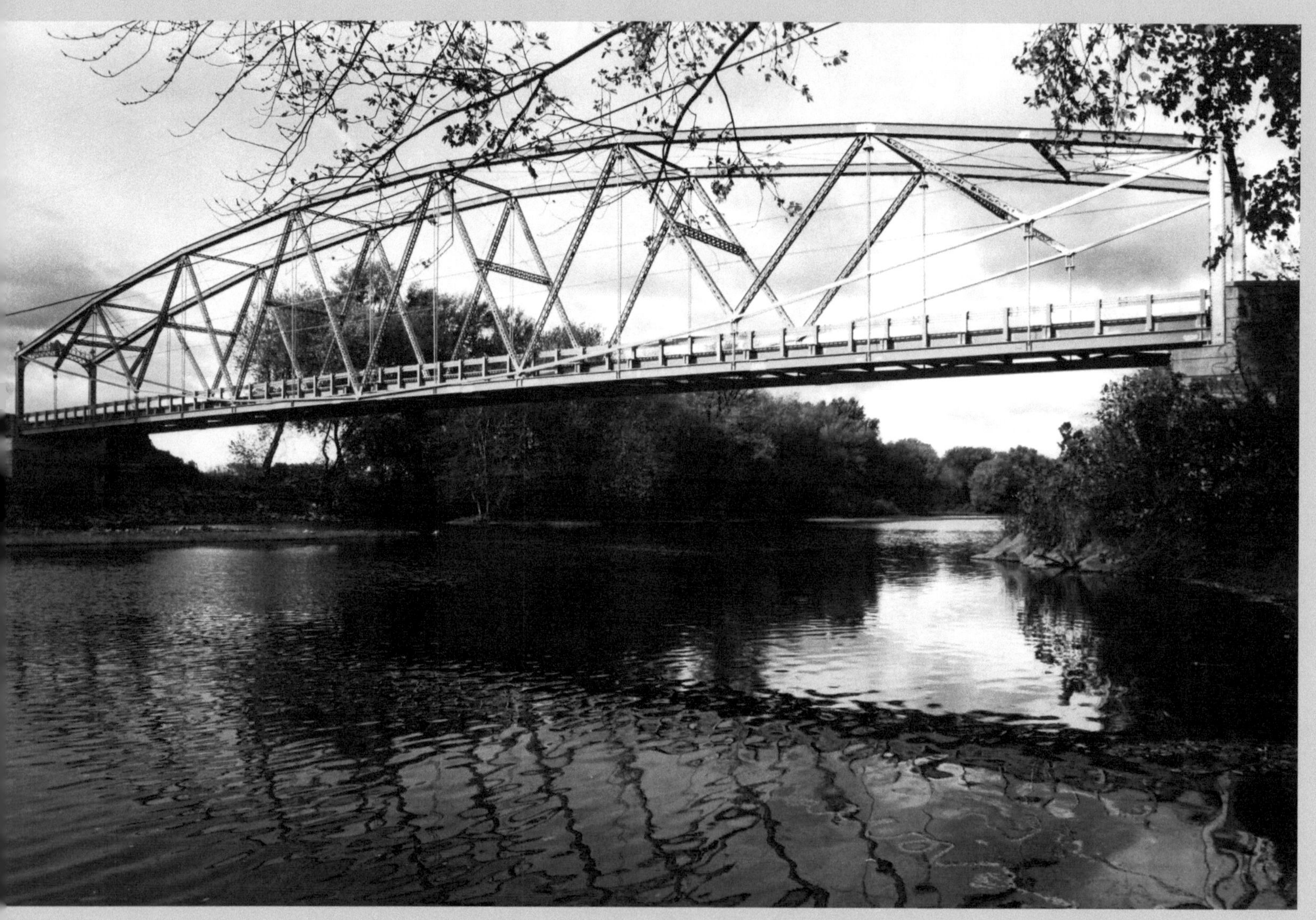

13-4803-18

The Pine Creek Bridge is a well-preserved example of the *lenticular* truss design manufactured at the Berlin Iron Bridge Company of Berlin, Connecticut. Lenticular refers to the truss shape resembling an optical lens's cross-section. The engineering record lists steel as the material used at Pine Creek, but I bet there are, or originally were, iron parts in the bridge. Steel was still in its early years of implementation in 1889, the year the bridge was built, and the manufacturer still called itself an "iron" bridge company.

Lenticular truss bridges were sold as "kits," with the parts made at the factory and then transported for assembly on site. The configuration of the internal trusswork seemed to vary between bridges; the Pine Creek example is a *Warren* truss with the signature "W" shaped diagonals clearly displayed. The bridge has a curious toy-like appearance, and its single span is striking and memorable. It was a beautiful and quiet day when my wife and I visited the bridge, and I can't remember encountering a passing car while there. It was like a bridge meditation while wading in the creek to get a nice picture.

This completes the Susquehanna River West Branch. Next, we pick the main branch in Upstate New York and visit several more lenticular truss bridges.

I can't do better than this in capturing an antique truss bridge with black+white film in a 50-year-old camera; this is as good as it gets. I've taken more atmospheric shots, but this one substantiates what it's like to behold a lenticular truss. It's called the Ouaquaga Bridge, after the town in New York where it is located. Kudos to the streets and road officials who preserved the bridge for bicycle and pedestrian use because a new bridge stands a few yards out of view, and, no doubt, the word "demolition" came up at least once in the planning meetings.

This bridge was built in 1888, a year before the Pine Creek Bridge, by the same company in Berlin, Connecticut. The engineer's drawings for this bridge can be viewed online, along with the patent drawings for the lenticular design. As a professional artist who sculpts and draws, I can assure my readers that we are *not* improving as a species with the conceits of advancing intelligence and creativity. The early Machine Age expressions that came off the ink-splattered desk of typical engineers of the time far exceed the computer-addled milquetoast we moderns pretend to call progressive. Instead of looking in the mirror, we should look over our shoulders for self-evaluation.

The Ouaquaga Bridge is a photogenic bridge with easy access to nearly perfect viewing points in the immediate vicinity. I wish all bridges were this easy. I visited the bridge more than once and tried to capture the feel of the area. The following page has a photo with this goal in mind.

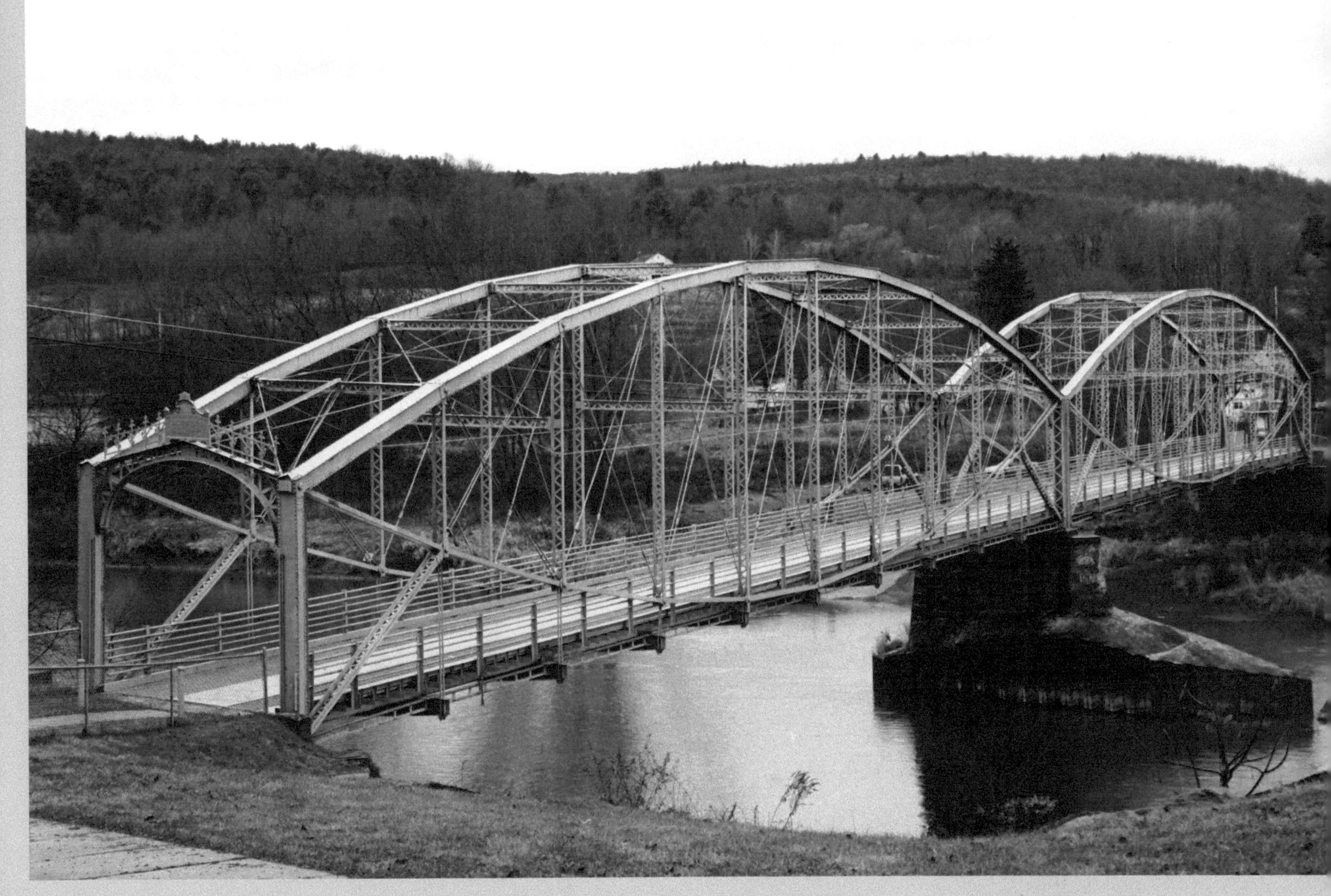

13-4813-09

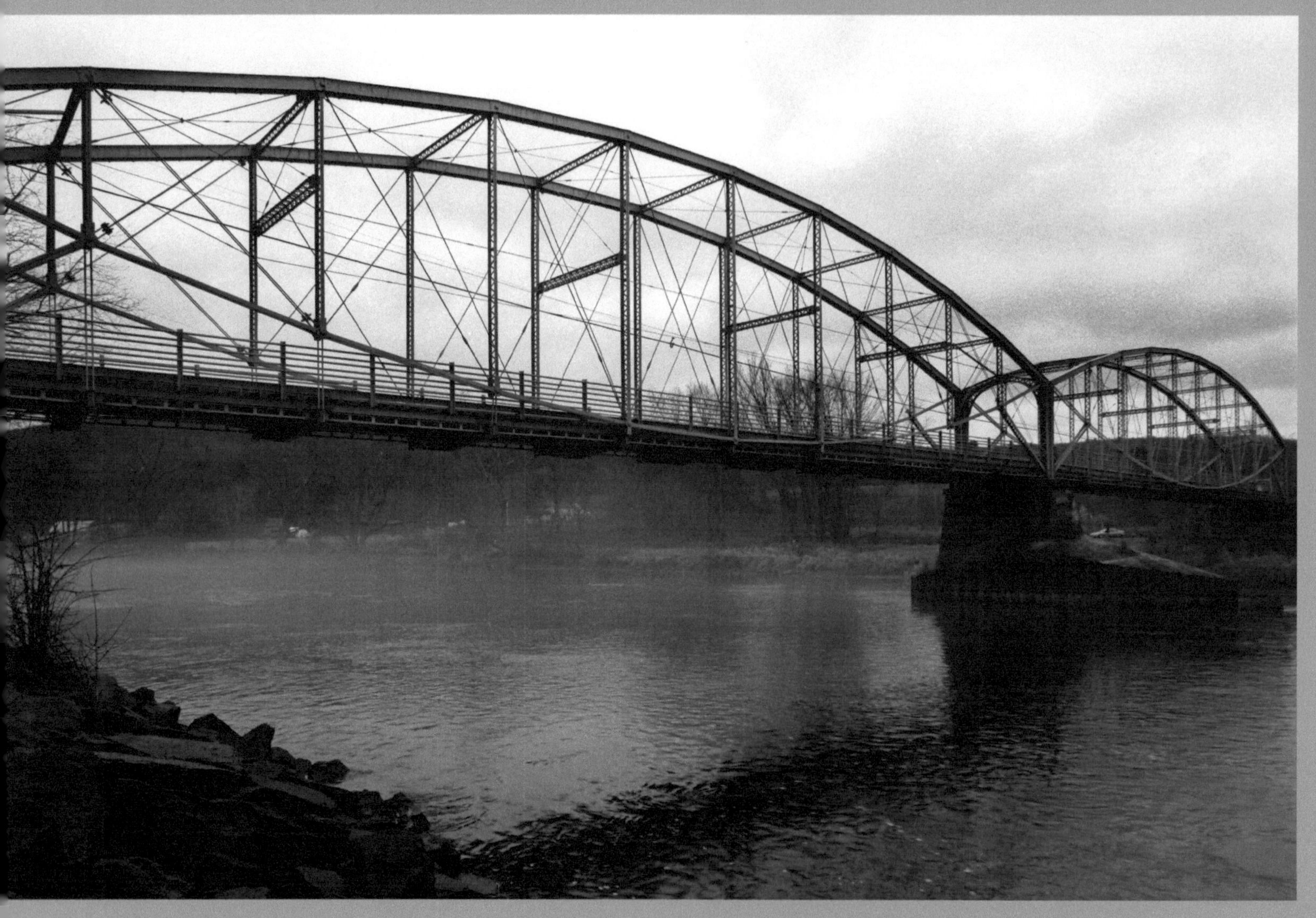

13-4810-14

Here's an atmospheric picture of the Ouaquaga Bridge. The upper waters of the Susquehanna look nothing like what we see in Pennsylvania; this is a photo of a bridge over a creek, not a major river. Joan accompanied me on this outing; we both like Upstate New York. It is a rugged place with people like those I encounter in a place like Ohio, with neither Appalachian nor East Coast temperaments, and where the girl behind the counter will say, “Thank you for your service,” to an armed forces vet or policeman.

However, on the day I took this photo, my romantic view of the region was disturbed by a pedestrian that watched me as I stood behind my camera, waiting for him to finish crossing the bridge. He didn't take his eyes off me as he walked up and asked if my camera had recorded his presence. I said “no,” which is the case because I'm not interested in photographing people. Joan watched from a distance, picked up the same thing I did from this guy, and was glad the exchange ended without incident. I don't know who or what he was, but I'm sure he ain't someone from Ohio.

In the photo, the bridge cuts the gray sky with the delicate lines of steel that I'm fond of capturing on film. The thin-wired tension elements and the thick verticle compression members easily define the distinctions between tension and compression pathways. Also, the thick and stiff *over-arching* top chord is clearly distinguishable from the thin *under-arching* bottom chord, which is the signature charm and elegance of the lenticular truss design.

Binghampton is our next New York stop, where a grander lenticular truss crosses the Susquehanna River.

Looking through records and photos of the South Washington Street Bridge made me realize everybody and his brother stood on the same concrete slab I found on the shoreline near the bridge. With Binghampton in the background, it's a nice view. It also captures the growing width and volume of the Susquehanna as it gathers strength along its passage across the Mid-Atlantic region.

The South Washington Street Bridge was completed in 1886, with three lenticular trusses constructed by the Berlin Iron Bridge Company of East Berlin, Connecticut. In 1969, the bridge was closed to all vehicular traffic and today stands as a well-preserved pedestrian crossing. It's a museum piece understood to have value as a civic and historical relic.

From here, our journey follows the river south and back into Pennsylvania, where we look at more antique trusses. We'll see our last Susquehanna bridge in Northumberland, before turning to New York City, where the atmosphere shifts from Appalachian hinterlands to densely urban. In the photographic context, the change is abrupt and couldn't be more profound.

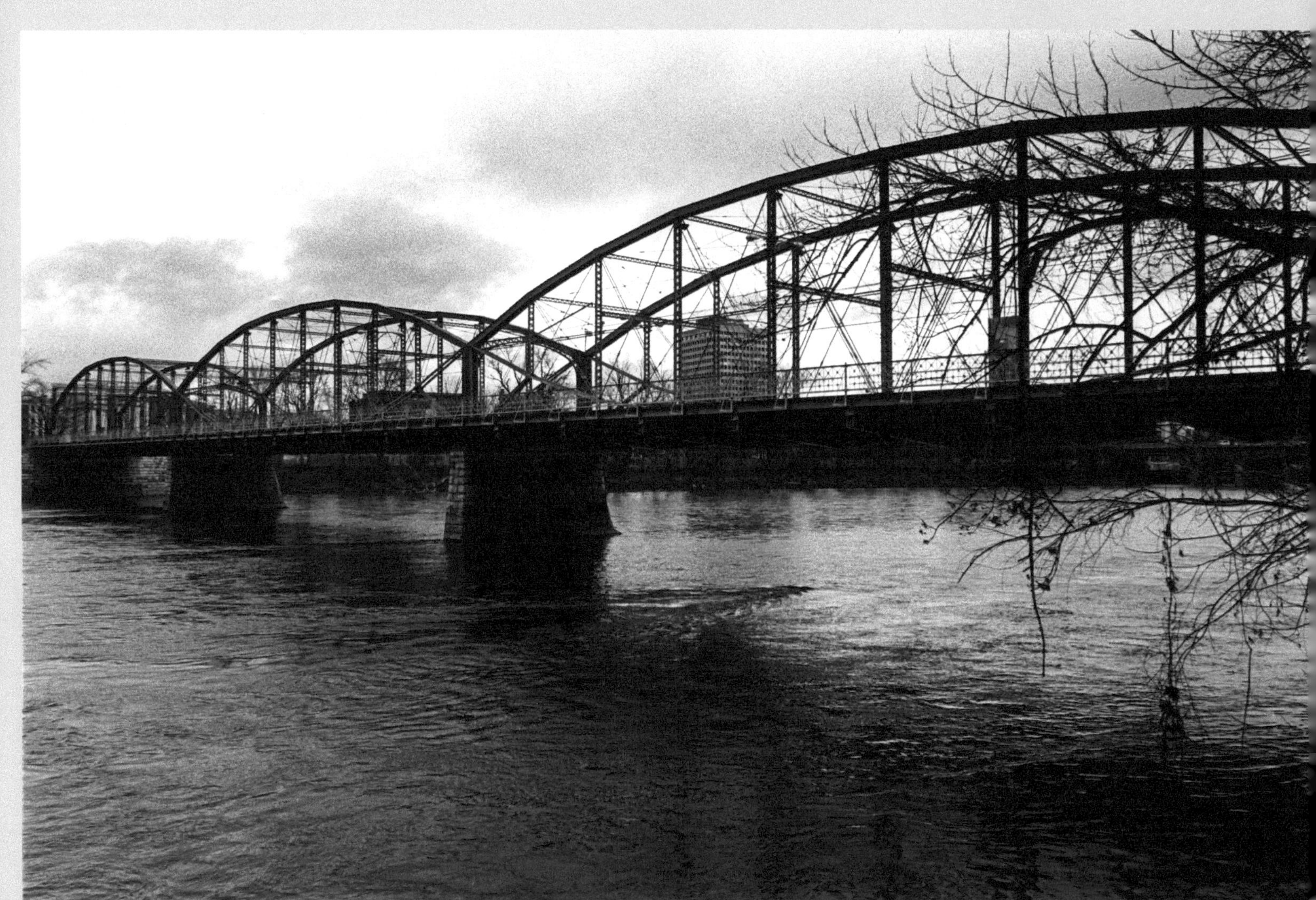

11-4637-09

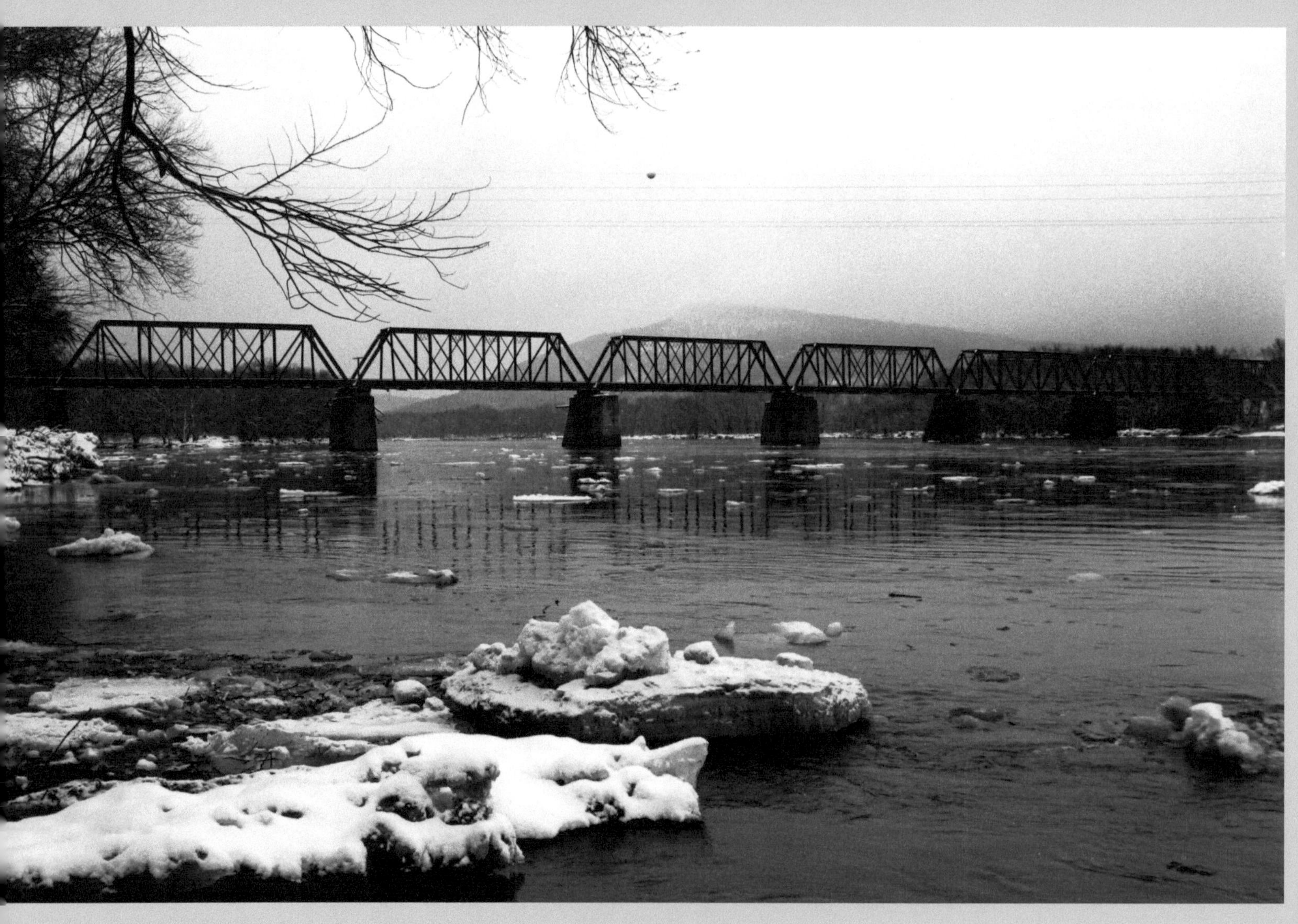

15-4907-05

15-4907-28 Overleaf

Page 56 and the overleaf have photos of the LSX Susquehanna River Bridge in Pittston, PA. Multiple *Pratt* trusses mix with subtle winter atmospherics and water reflections, making photography easy on that cold January afternoon.

I'm not a train nut, per se, but I can't get enough of these railroad bridge masterpieces that occupy the banks of the Susquehanna River. We're looking at monuments from a period of human history that indulged the optimistic expressions of conquering nature and gravity with a puritanical restraint that presaged the High Modernist notion of *form follows function*, which later dominated our era in architecture and design. Artists of the 20th Century, consciously or unconsciously, absorbed and imitated the linear forms and repetition of the structural engineer in the same way rock and roll music mimicked the pulse and drone of machines on the factory floor. Yes, life imitates art; but art imitates the practical realities of its age, sometimes for the better and sometimes for the worst. Ambiguity is the ultimate spice of life; the barefooted artist is the hapless cook that tries to find the right recipe.

The following pages are a medley of various simple truss spans for highway and railroad, completing our Susquehanna menu before changing hats and going total urban as we hit the streets of NYC, Easton, and Philadelphia with a side trip to New Jersey.

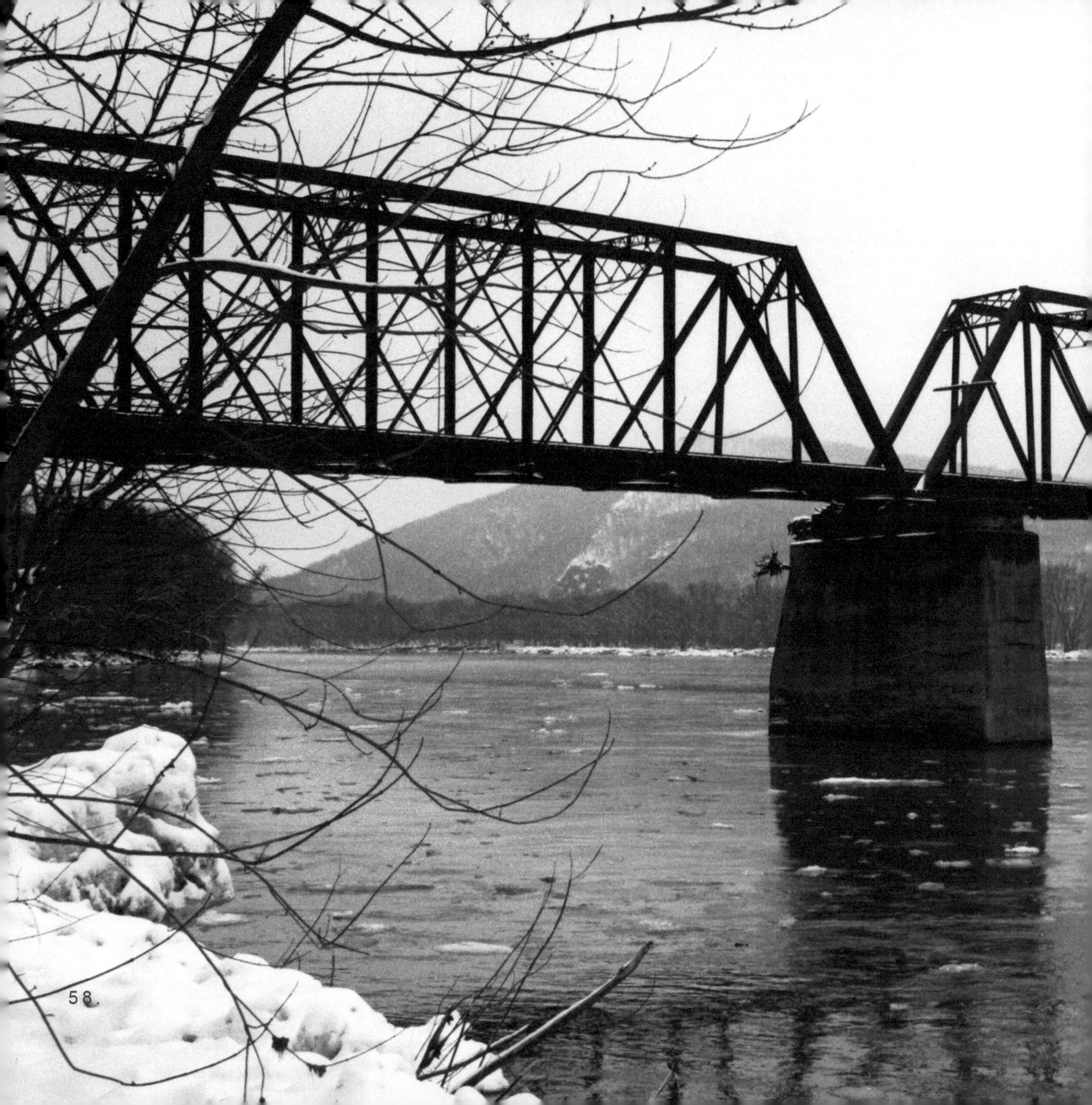

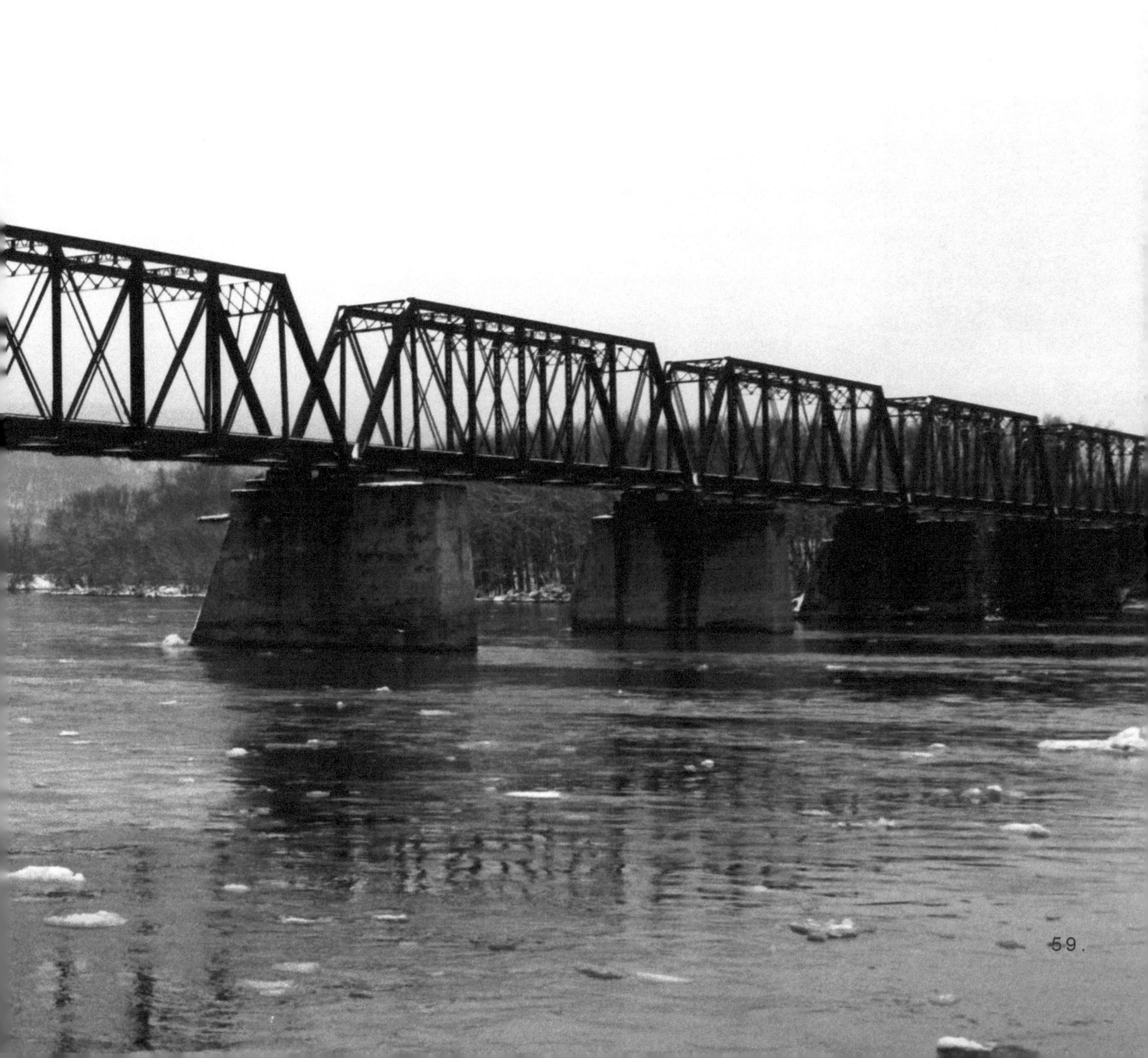

The Nanticoke Bridge consists of three truss spans; two are *Pennsylvania* trusses, and one is a weird combination of *Pennsylvania* and *Parker* trusses. I've never seen anything like this. The story behind this odd configuration isn't well understood. The two possibilities I got from ***HistoricBridges.org*** involve differentials in load bearing during traffic or issues with railroad tracks that passed under the bridge during its construction back in 1914. Either way, it's a mysterious bridge in the annals of bridge design and construction.

From where I stood photographing the Nanticoke Bridge, I pivoted my camera left 45 degrees and captured the Nanticoke Railroad Bridge. Pictured on the overleaf, it's a span of multiple *Warren* trusses. The bridges, highways, and towns along this stretch of the Susquehanna share a lot with the Paleozoic geology of the river and surrounding hills; everything looks old, including the people and the culture. Often, the banks of the Susquehanna are veins of Appalachia cutting into the more progressive Mid-Atlantic territory. It's an ancient wound that confounds politicians, officials, and anyone with enough knowledge of anthropology to detect it. Most travelers unconsciously press their car's accelerator and give the place no further thought.

Pennsylvania has more miles of road per square mile of land than any other state in America; it also has more towns per mile than anywhere else. In our final years as active professional artists, Joan and I have settled into a pattern of staying local, committing to Pennsylvania what we once did using half the continent. So far, it's a gamble that has worked; the village response has been nothing less than astounding. The future is in the hinterland; buy early and save.

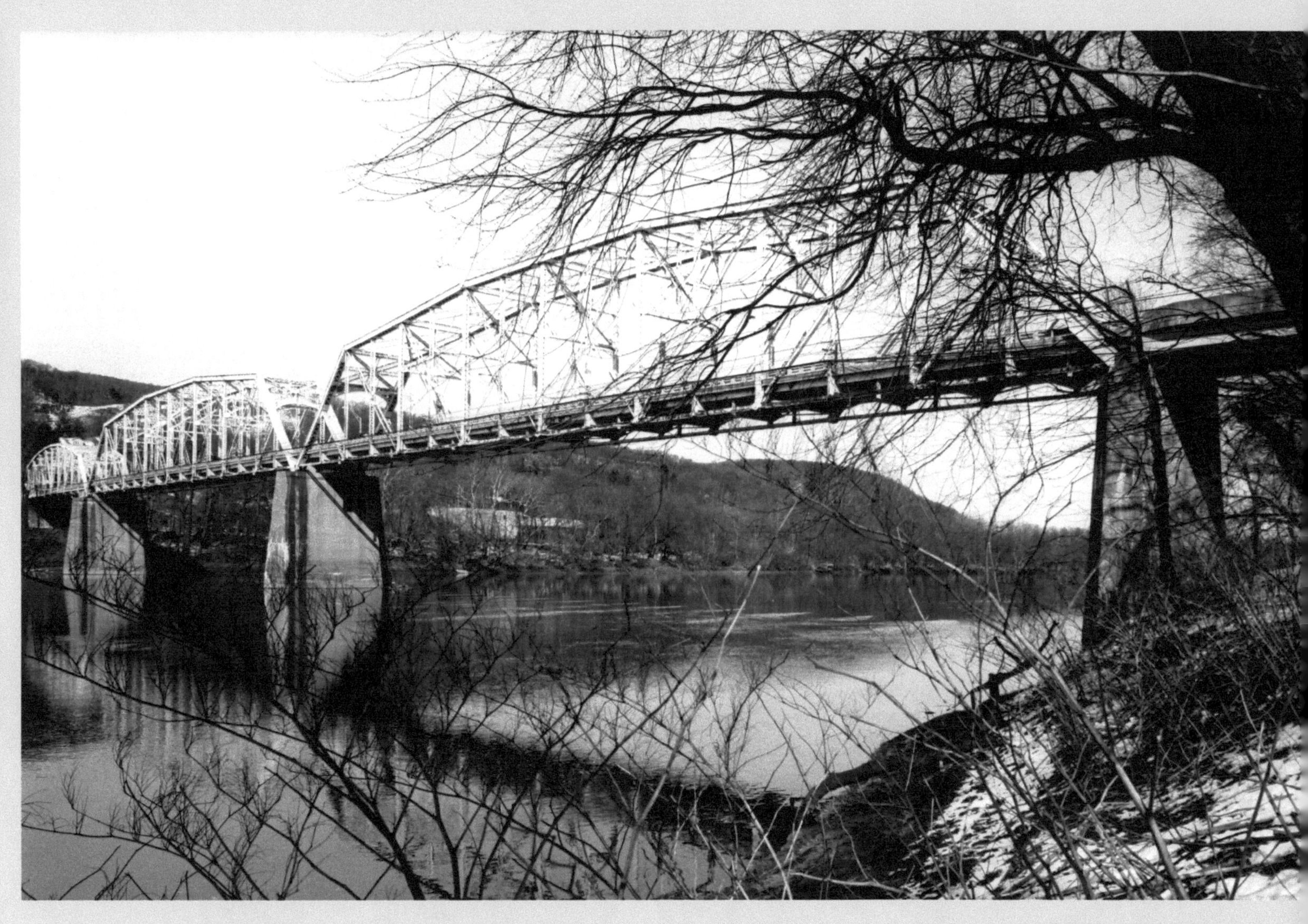

17-4966-14

Overleaf 17-4966-36

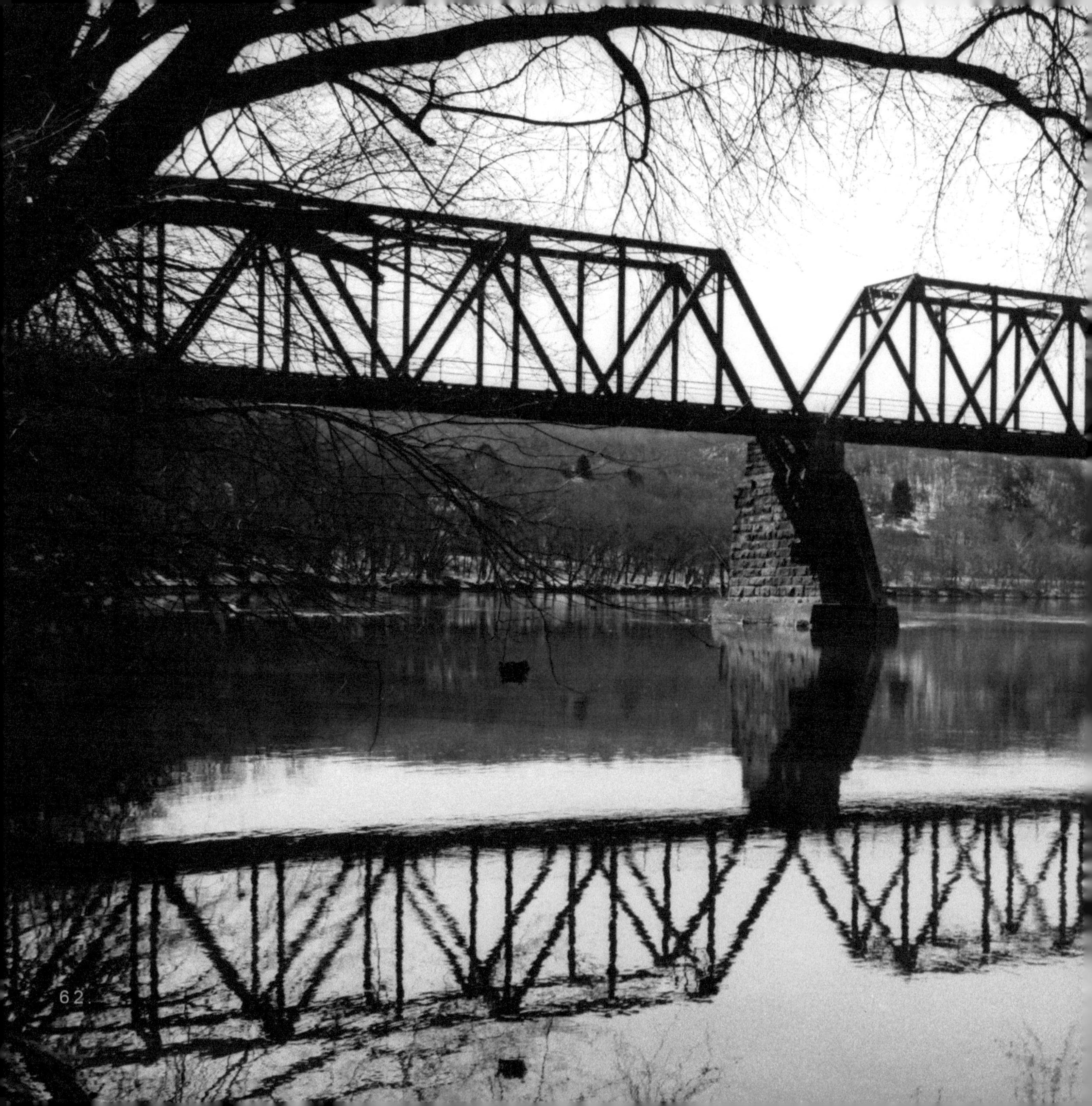

62.

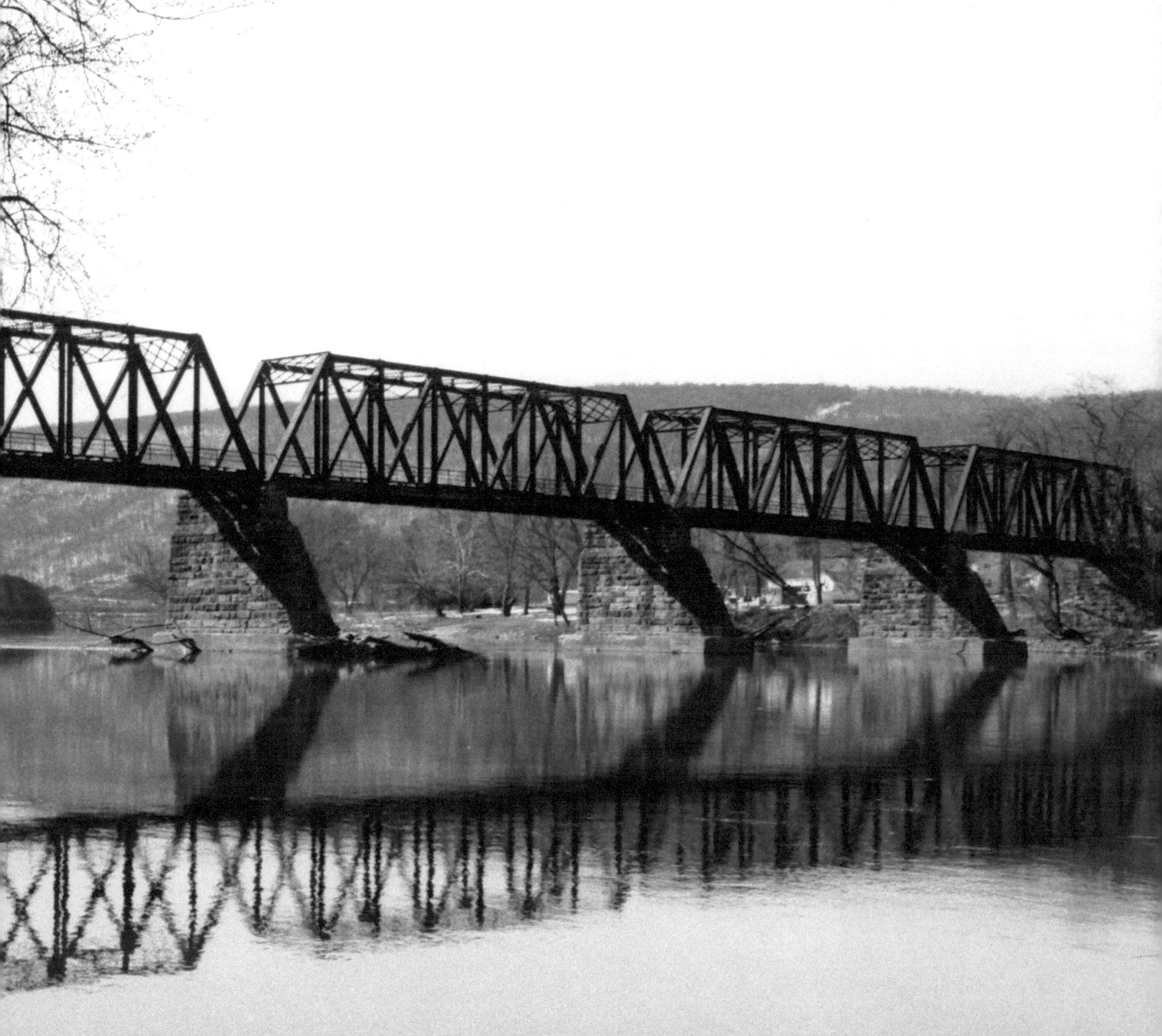

63.

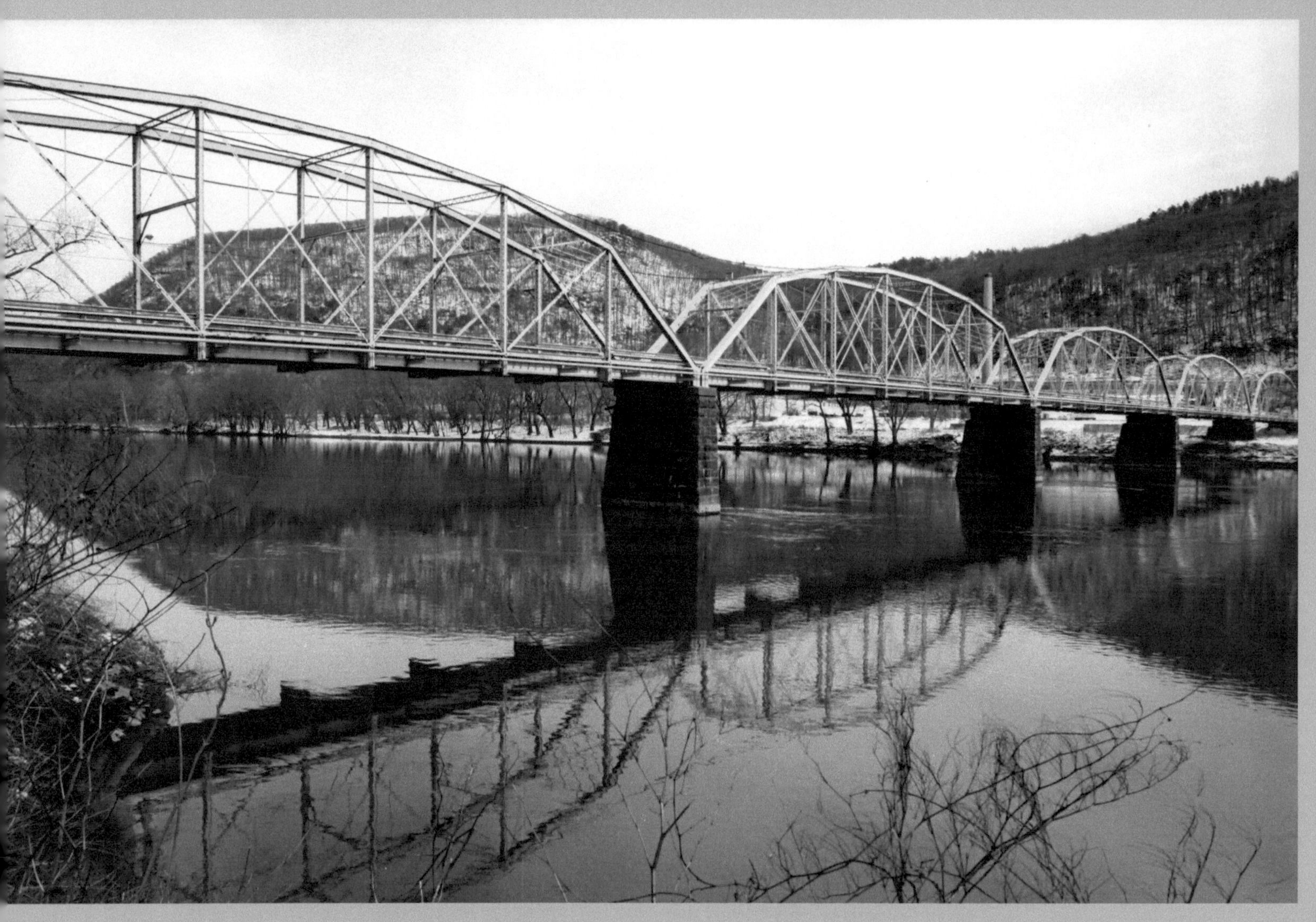

17-4967-21

On page 64 is a nice photo of five *Parker* truss spans. The Parker design is a *Pratt* configuration with a curved top chord; the diagonals "V" toward the bottom/center then overlap, forming an "X" in the middle. The thin diagonals carry the tension forces, and the robust vertical members are in compression.

They call it the Retreat Access Road Bridge, a very polite way of describing a bridge that goes to a prison campus. Joan and I often pass the place while taking the back road to Wilkes-Barre, and the bridge was on my to-do list for years. On a calm and windless day in February, I finally pulled off the road with my cameras. Secured facilities can attract unwanted attention when the camera and tripod are deployed, but nothing happened that day. I've heard the place is now closed.

The bridge has a storied past. It was removed from its original location in Plymouth, PA, and re-assembled in the present spot in the early 1950s. Its current status is undoubtedly still being determined, defying the propensity of the roads and bridge officials to demolish old bridges. We hope it stays put.

The Packers Island Bridge is our last stop on the Susquehanna River. The bridge is called a *camelback* truss, recognized by five segments forming the arch configuration of the top chord; other types have seven or more. Packers Island is located where the West Branch joins the Susquehanna in Sunbury, PA. We've completed a loop beginning in Maryland, north into Appalachia, and from New York State south through parts of the Mid-Atlantic, back to where we started. We live on an old farm in the bullseye of this circular path, and we frequently pass some of these bridges in our everyday travels.

During my time as a substitute teacher, I passed Packer Island on my way to Sunbury. I was called there often, and being around the kids of the region taught me a lot about the culture. Sunbury isn't far from the coal mining districts, another frequent school destination. I was advised to avoid these classrooms; the coal towns are the poorest in Pennsylvania and the kids are tough.

For three years, I worked in the coal region at a food warehouse, and many of my co-workers lived in Sunbury. After paying child-support and working lots of overtime, these guys had little left to live on. I had absolutely no idea how they got by each month, and this is coming from someone used to penny pinching while living off of art sales, which are hardly regular. Sunbury and the adjacent coal region form a vortex in rural Pennsylvania, that which James Carville called the "Alabama" between Philadelphia and Pittsburgh, and I'm calling Appalachia.

I was open about hating my warehouse job; I loudly cursed at my boss and slammed the door on the lunchroom crowd, eating alone in a locked kitchen. My abject honesty won me the trust of the entire warehouse, which was far from my intent. I became the local bartender; I listened to everyone's stories. I looked at cell phone pictures of fish tanks and the aquatic occupants, hamburgers from Friday night's restaurant dinner with pornography for dessert, and a dilapidated camper that will go camping someday.

And they pestered me to hear my art stories. Mine differed: tales from the D.C. Beltway, New York's Upper West Side, Lincoln Park Chicago, or accounts from houses with moats keeping out Cleveland or Detroit. They wanted to hear what happened after being buzzed through a high iron gate that led to rooms with yet higher ceilings. They wanted to know what I said to spoiled kids with an even more spoiled mother who used body language that made a married artist nervous. They tried to find out what it's like to take a beverage from the hands of a dark-skinned Guatemalan housegirl, feeling like an extra in a medieval plot line. They listened to my words as we stood outside the warehouse surveillance cameras.

Ok, now it's time for NYC.

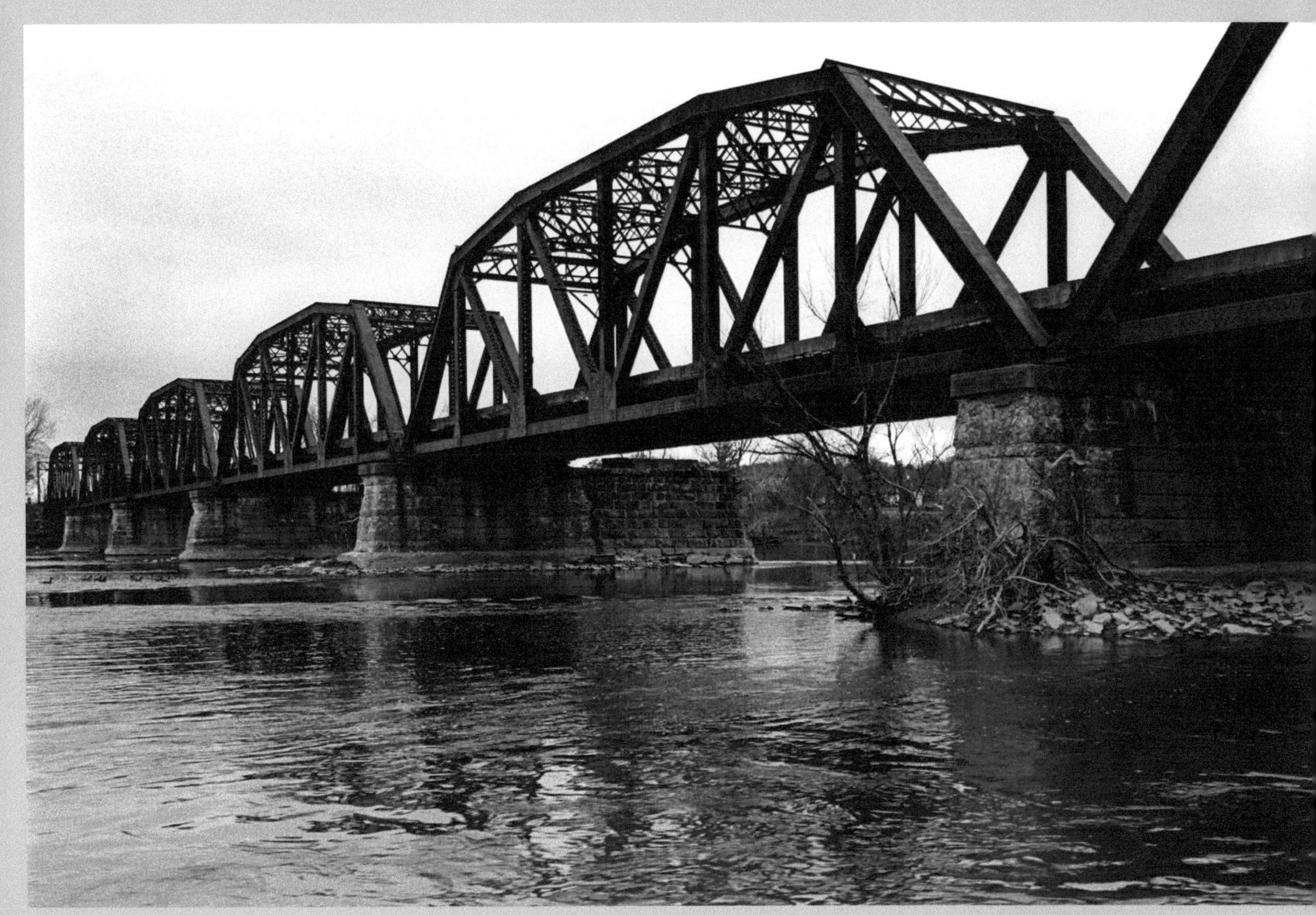

12-4648-15

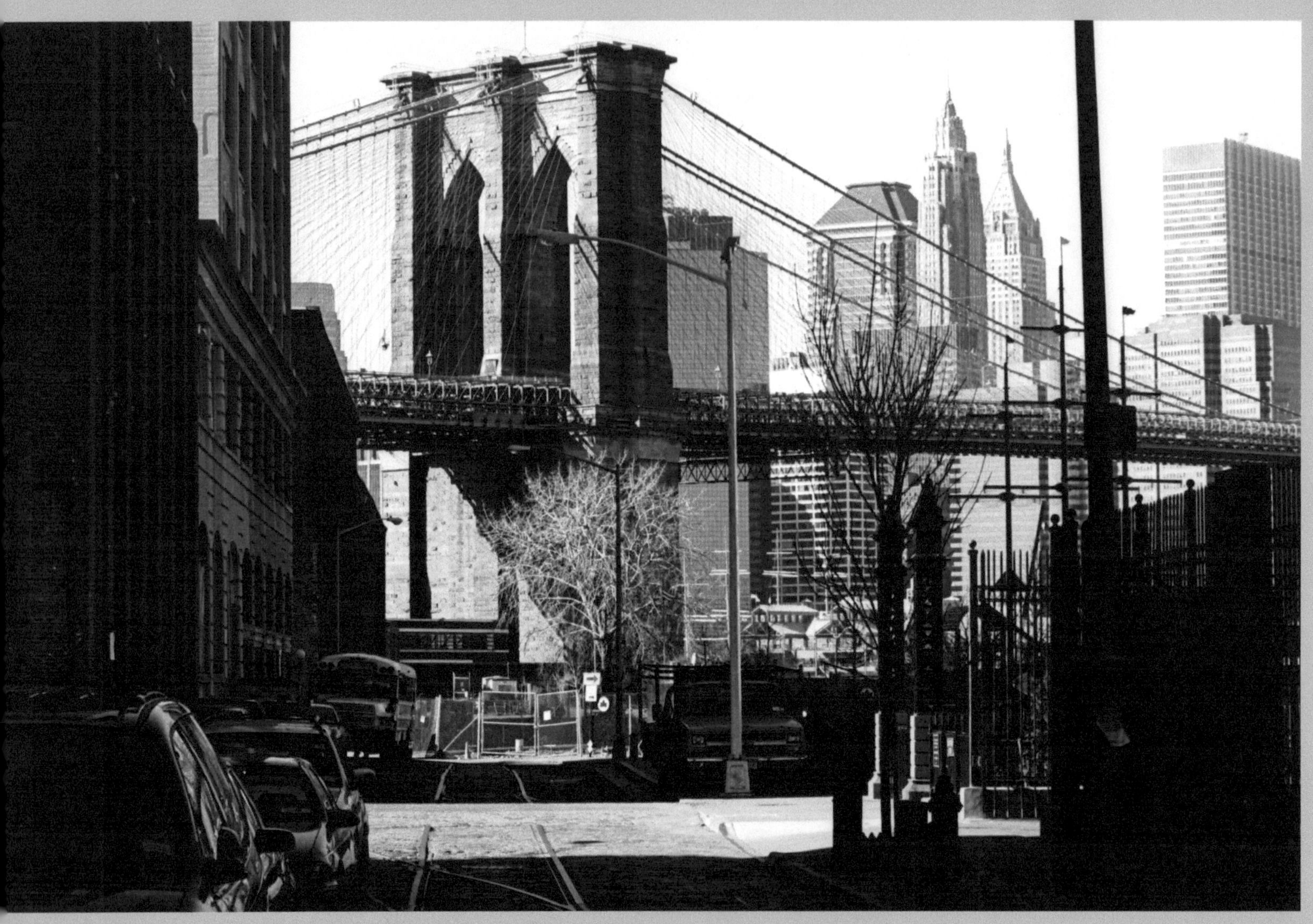

02-6811-16

New York City is where it's possible to attach a broken camera to the back of my pants, rattle around the streets, and get good pictures; somehow, the textures, shadows, and planes converge and form harmonious compositions. It's magic I don't understand and used to my advantage on several trips to the city. The Brooklyn Bridge photo on page 68 was from a few months after 9-11, and I remember feeling I should get up there before things got more clamped down, making bridge gazing risky. Since that time, I've been warned by fellow infrastructure enthusiasts to keep away from such things in North Jersey and NYC; there are tales of cameras being confiscated. Since that September day, things have never been the same.

The Brooklyn Bridges is so much a part of our cultural currency that almost everyone has one in the back pocket to sell to hapless pollyannas. The bridge's history has been repeated in books and documentaries, so I'm not going to add to the noise except to mention a structural design detail I find most interesting.

Arguably, the Brooklyn Bridge is a *hybrid* of two configurations; the *suspension* and the *cable-stayed*. The suspension bridge design is familiar to generations of road travelers and is what is typically assigned to the Brooklyn Bridge. On the other hand, the cable-stayed is becoming more familiar and is the design of choice for most new construction, at least since the turn of the 21st Century. Cable-stays refer to the gossamer thin cables radiating from the crest of the stone towers, overlapping the vertical suspender cables to produce the optical effect that captures our attention for its graphic elegance. The Brooklyn Bridge is a three-dimensional drawing that transcribes to black+white films very well.

I'm assigning the adjective "arguably" to the bridge's shared configuration because it's unclear how John Roebling intended the conjunction approaches to make the bridge stand. What isn't arguable is that it worked. Also, there is no argument that the primary tension forces are channeled in the large cables. Still, significant tension is in the cable-stays, making them at least measurable as stabilizers for reducing oscillation arising from traffic and wind forces. Presumably, engineers with their digital computers have settled the issue. But I don't want to hear any of it; my pleasure comes from analog speculation. I'm an artist first and only when thinking about these things.

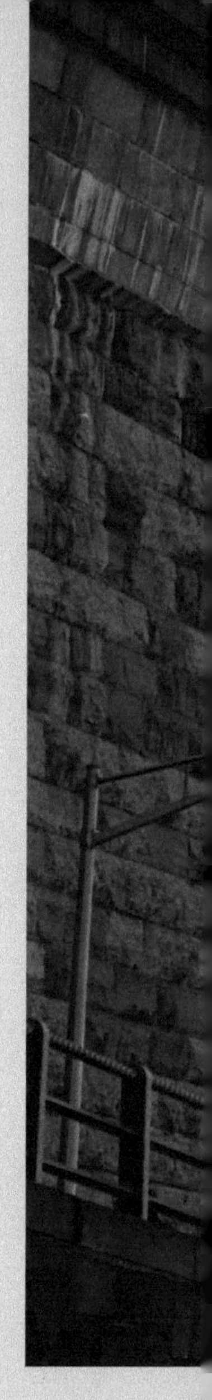

02-6812-02

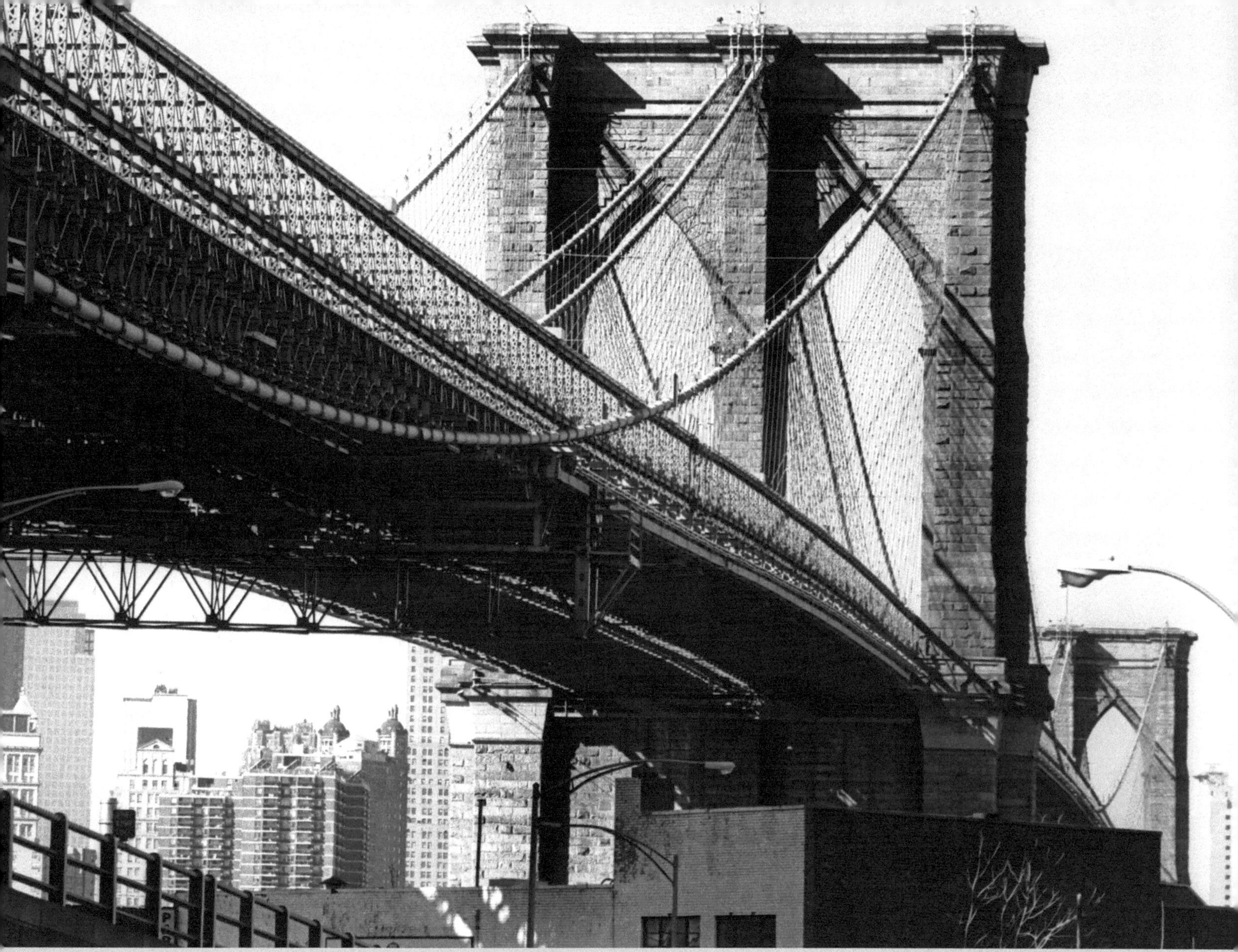

71.

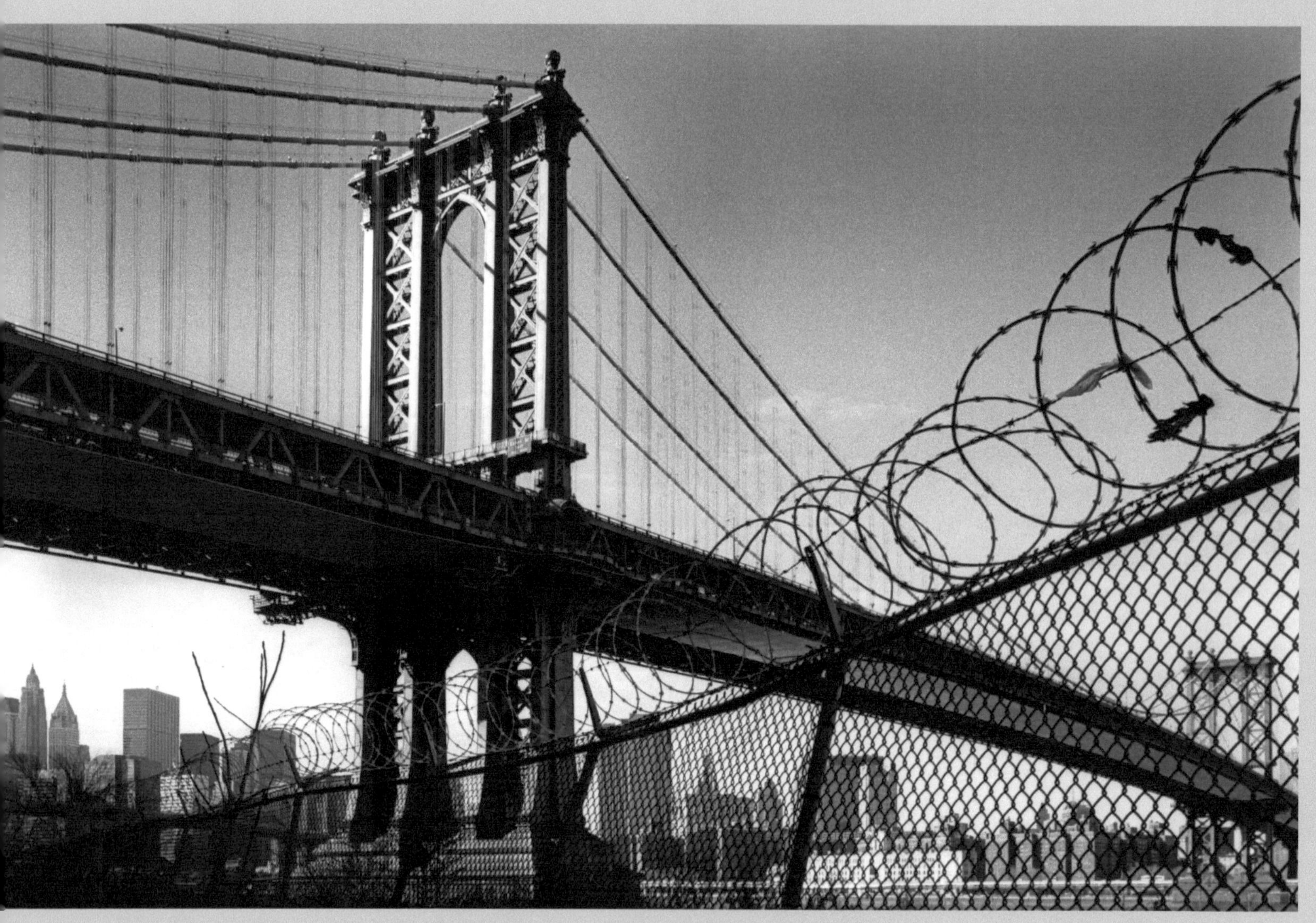

02-6809-30

The first person to purchase my photograph of the Manhattan Bridge said he was doing so because he was interested in prisons. Okay? As long as your check is good, I don't care. The idea of razor wire intrigued him, he claimed; and that's the wonder of art. Without ambiguity, it ain't art, so a picture of a bridge can be art. In fact, most significantly, a picture of a bridge can be art because it means taking a utilitarian object and framing it to be perceived as both beautiful and practical, and with the addition of razor wire, menacing.

In the case of the Manhattan Bridge, ambiguity was designed into the bridge; nothing emerged from the drafting room without explicit attention to grace and beauty. The modernist precept of *form follows function* was matched with a certain latitude to include ornamentation, giving the bridge an Old World feel.

Bookmark this notion while we complete Volume 2, especially as we travel into the middle of the continent in Volume 3. Ornamentation fades as the modernist aesthetic matures completely, yet unconsciously, in the infinite space of the American Great Plains. It took a particular German traveler who recognized something in American grain silos, brought it back to Europe, and birthed the age of modern design.

Pages 74+75 have another view of the Manhattan Bridge. It's a sidewalk photo rich with textures and shadows.

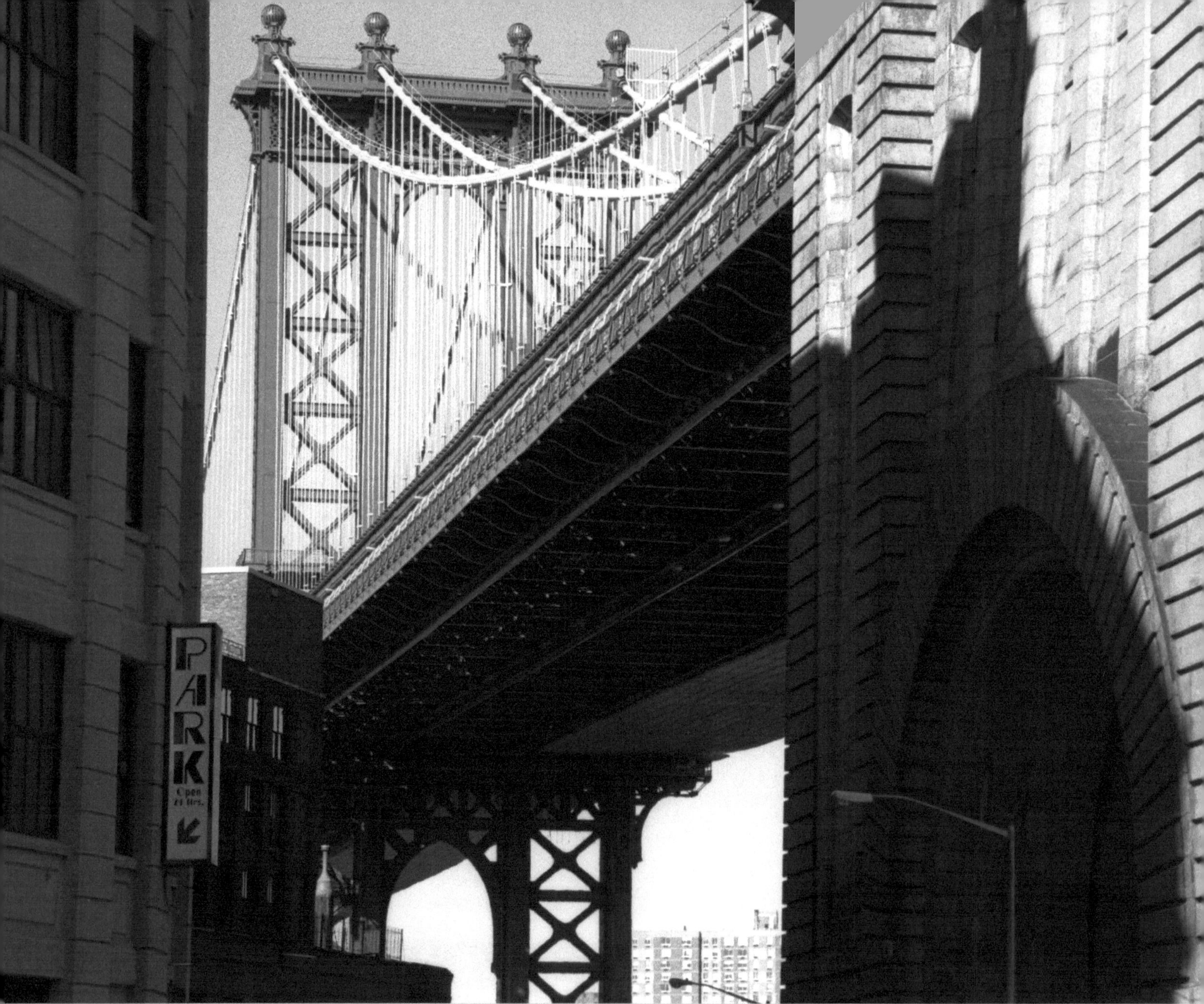


74.

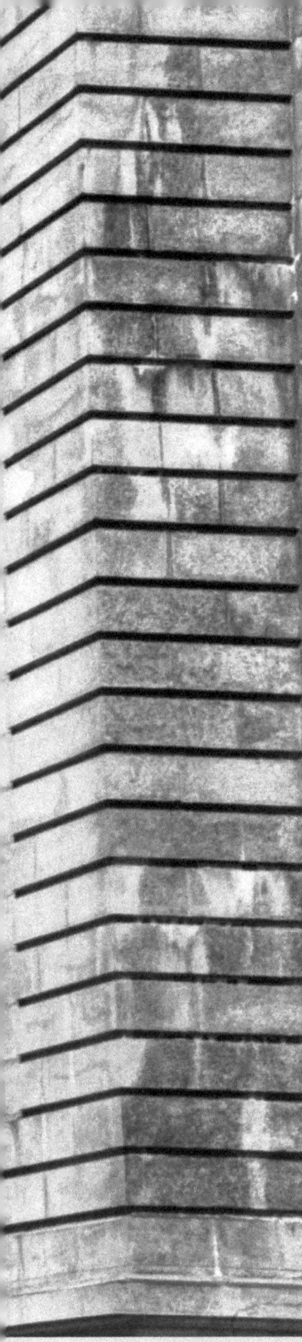

02-6810-07

The Queensboro Bridge is a cantilever truss of magnificent mass and scale, designed with double-deck roadways that carry enough traffic to defy obsolescence well into the 21st Century. Finished in 1909 with supervision by a host of engineers under Gustav Lindenthal, the master of bridge design during his age.

I discussed at length the *cantilever* construction method in Volume 1. Still, I'll remind readers the central idea behind this type of bridge is the absence of falsework (scaffolding) supporting the nascent spans as they are assembled over the open waters. The bridge is built using itself as the support shelf as each section "grows" off the piers and joins in the middle to complete the span. Tension forces are carried by the upper chord. By looking carefully at the steel members gracefully curving down from the towers, they are discernably eyebars linked together in a chain, a common telltale sign we've located the tension pathway. The weakest and most dangerous point in the cantilever construction process is just before the halves meet. Both arms are swaying over the river, a few feet from joining in the middle. At this moment, the tension forces carried in the top chord are beyond imagination, and collapse is catastrophic if it happens, and it has. See the story of the Quebec Bridge Collapse; it happened just before construction was started on the Queensboro Bridge.

On this note, we complete our NYC stop and travel south, first into New Jersey, then completing Volume 2 on the Pennsylvania side of the Delaware River.

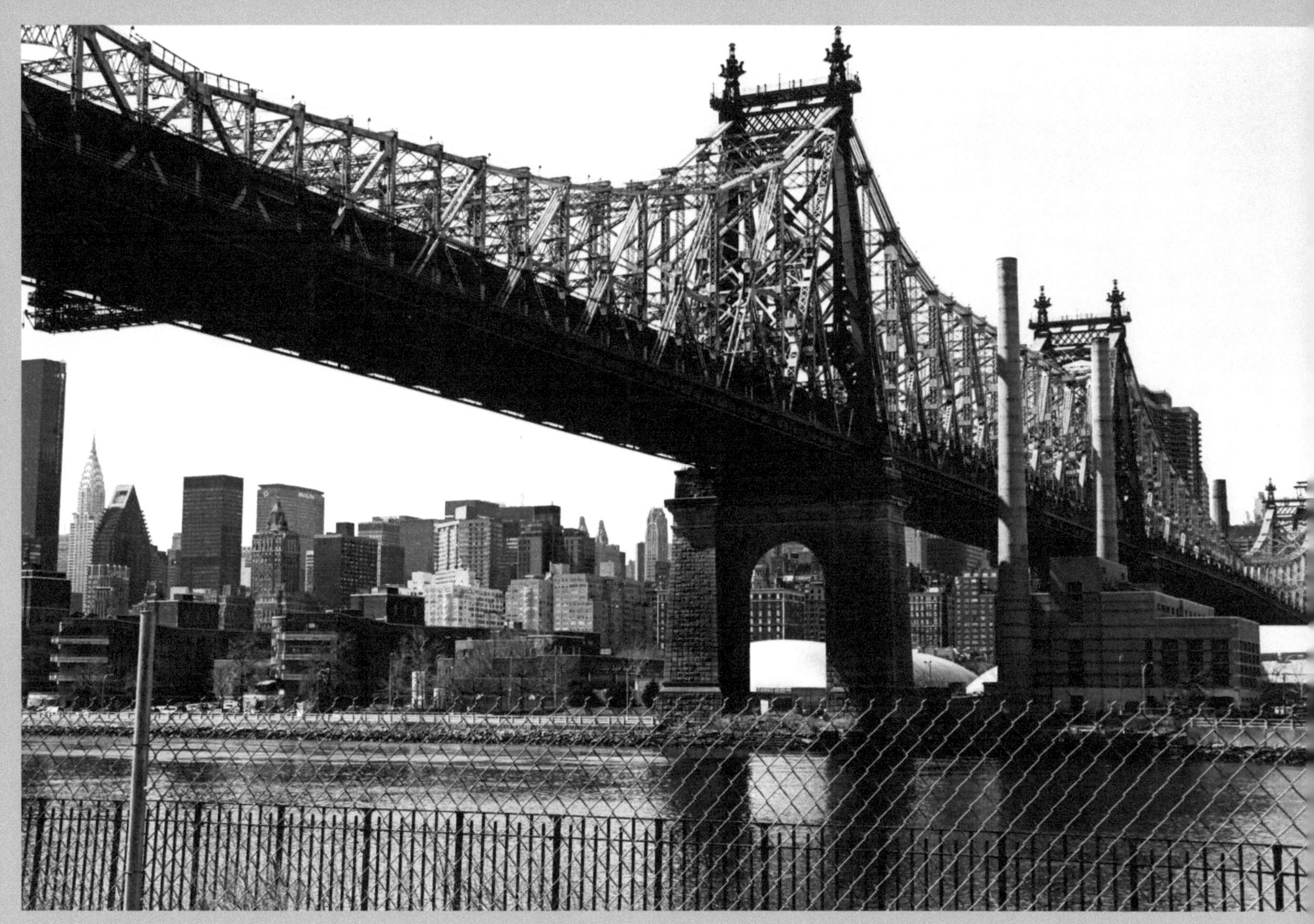

01-3955-31

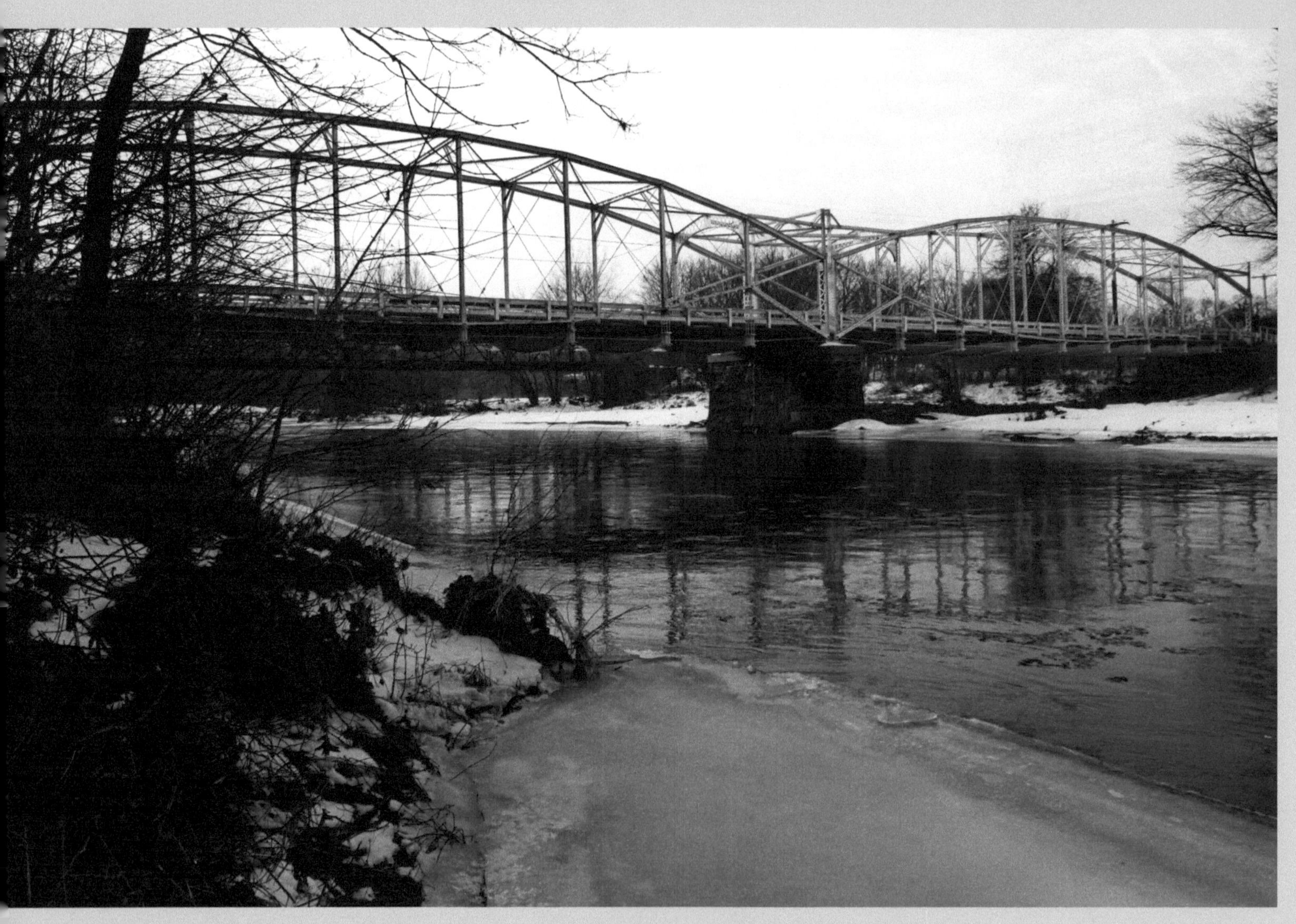

14-4834-25

14-4834-15 Overleaf

Page 78 and the overleaf have photos of the Neshanic Station Bridge, crossing the south branch of the Raritan River in New Jersey. The riverside spot I found to photograph the bridge is the same as everyone else found who came to admire and record their visit. My views differ by using black+white films and the antique outcomes I pursue.

I originally planned to publish only the first photo. Still, I added the overleaf view because of the surprising shift in lighting perspectives, with the difference in camera location measured in mere feet. Which is the better photo? I don't know. So, I give you both as an expression of literary and artistic license, courtesy of the self-publishing industry. Typically, a book editor would force a choice; that's what editors do.

The Neshanic Station Bridge is considered a historically significant structure and has been renovated many times since its construction in 1896. It retains many original details, even as the engineers have added safeguards to ensure vehicular safety. *Lenticular* truss bridges are now widely accepted as worthy of preservation. The Mid-Atlantic region is one of the best areas to find them.

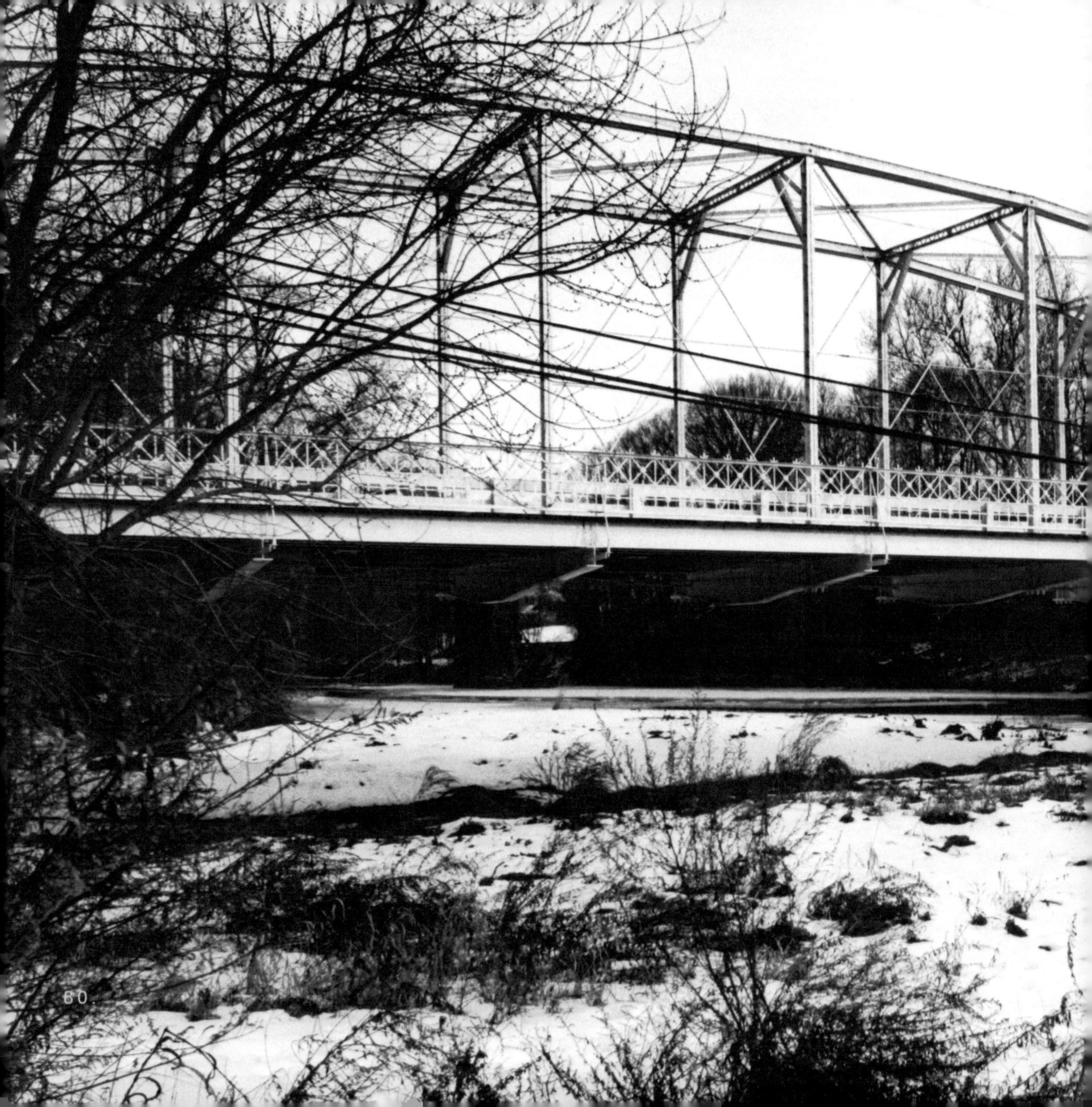

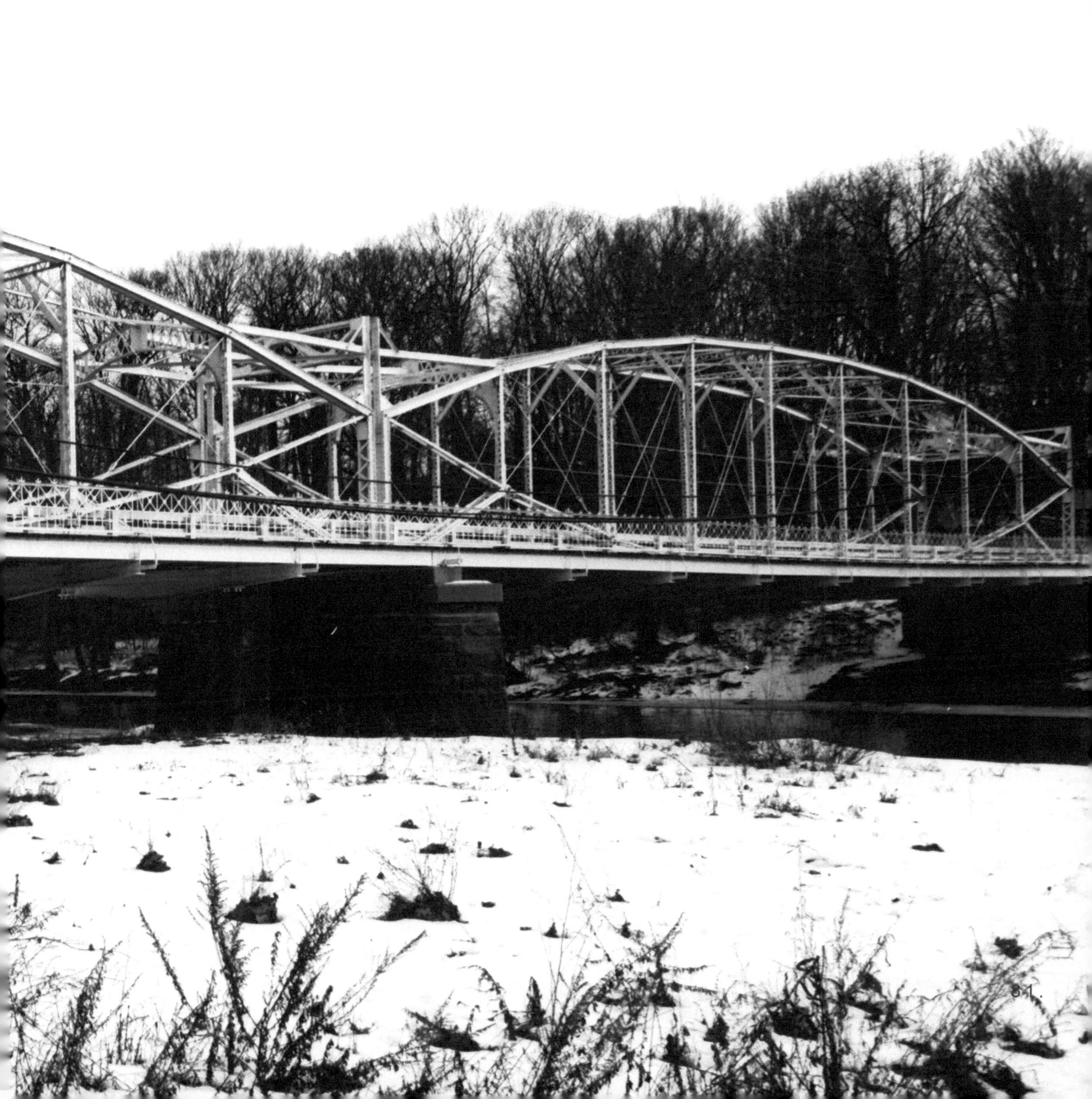

We now cross the Delaware River from New Jersey into the Lehigh Valley of Pennsylvania. This is an old and sprawling metropolitan area once anchored by the conspicuous presence of Bethlehem Steel with its many acres of smokestacks and foundry structures. All are gone except for an operating boutique foundry and a colossal park littered with steel-industry dinosaurs. We spend the rest of Volume 2 crunching across the broken glass and rusting archeology of the Lehigh Valley and moving southward along the Delaware River into Philadelphia as we explore the bridges that made sense here in times past.

Welcome to the post-modern dry bed and wasteland of the formerly great Mid-Atlantic powerhouses of labor and industry. Today, you may find rusty gears, tools, and forged fragments that characterized manual work embedded in thick, clear epoxy used as table-tops at craft breweries; nobody has a clue what they are or their use, nor does anyone care. With our combined decadence and insouciance, we are due a big spanking; something has to give as we park our asses atop a mound of privilege and an ahistorical understanding of what got us to this comfortable place. What is forgotten returns, fueled with a vengeance. Looking at antique steel bridges may jar our collective memory.

The Lehigh River 3rd Street Railroad Bridge, on page 83, crosses the concrete arched 3rd Street Bridge, creating a composition in space and time as the different design styles and materials mix with reflections and shadows. We are standing in Easton, PA, where the Lehigh River empties into the Delaware River.

The bridge photograph on the front cover of this volume is also in Easton and is called the Northampton Street Bridge, which crosses the Delaware River to New Jersey. I mistook this *cantilever* truss for an eyebar chain suspension bridge. Refer back to Volume 1, and the Three Sisters Bridges in Pittsburgh will explain my confusion. Both bridge types have a chain-linked eyebar top chord in tension. The difference is in the *vertical* members: the Three Sisters are eyebars in tension and are of thin stature; the Northampton Street verticals are thick, stiff, and in compression. Don't get too exercised if you're not following my words; this stuff becomes clear slowly after staring at these things over time.

The Lehigh and Hudson River Valley Railroad Bridge is downriver from the Northampton Street Bridge and is seen through the morning mist in the cover photo. We take a closer look at pages 84+85. This is a three-span Parker truss, where the diagonals "V" toward the bottom/center of each span, then cross over to make an "X" in the middle, and the top chord is curved. A detail, which sets this bridge apart from others, is the railroad path bends as it passes through the bridge, causing the end posts to skew, or "walk," into the curve. By looking carefully at the photo, you can see this detail revealed by the out-of-alignment appearance of the threshold where the train enters the bridge; it's subtle, so no worries if you miss this one.

Next, we go downriver to where the Pennsylvania Turnpike crosses over the Delaware River into New Jersey and look at our final span before entering Philadelphia.

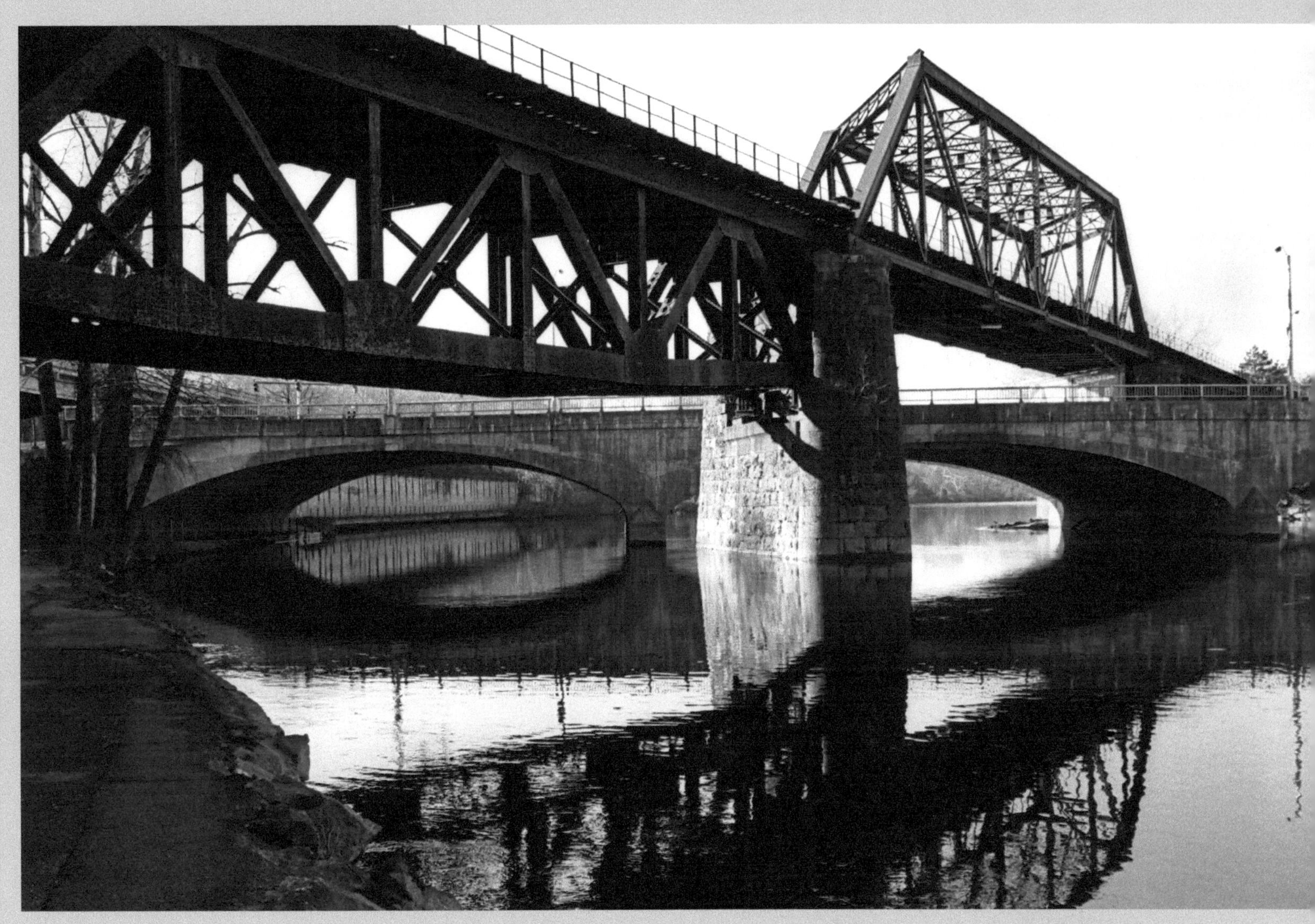

12-4641-08

12-4640-08

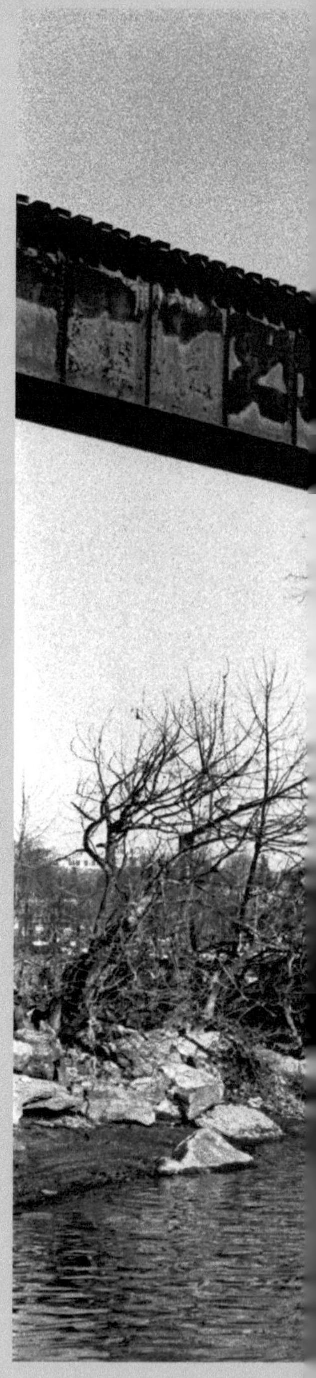

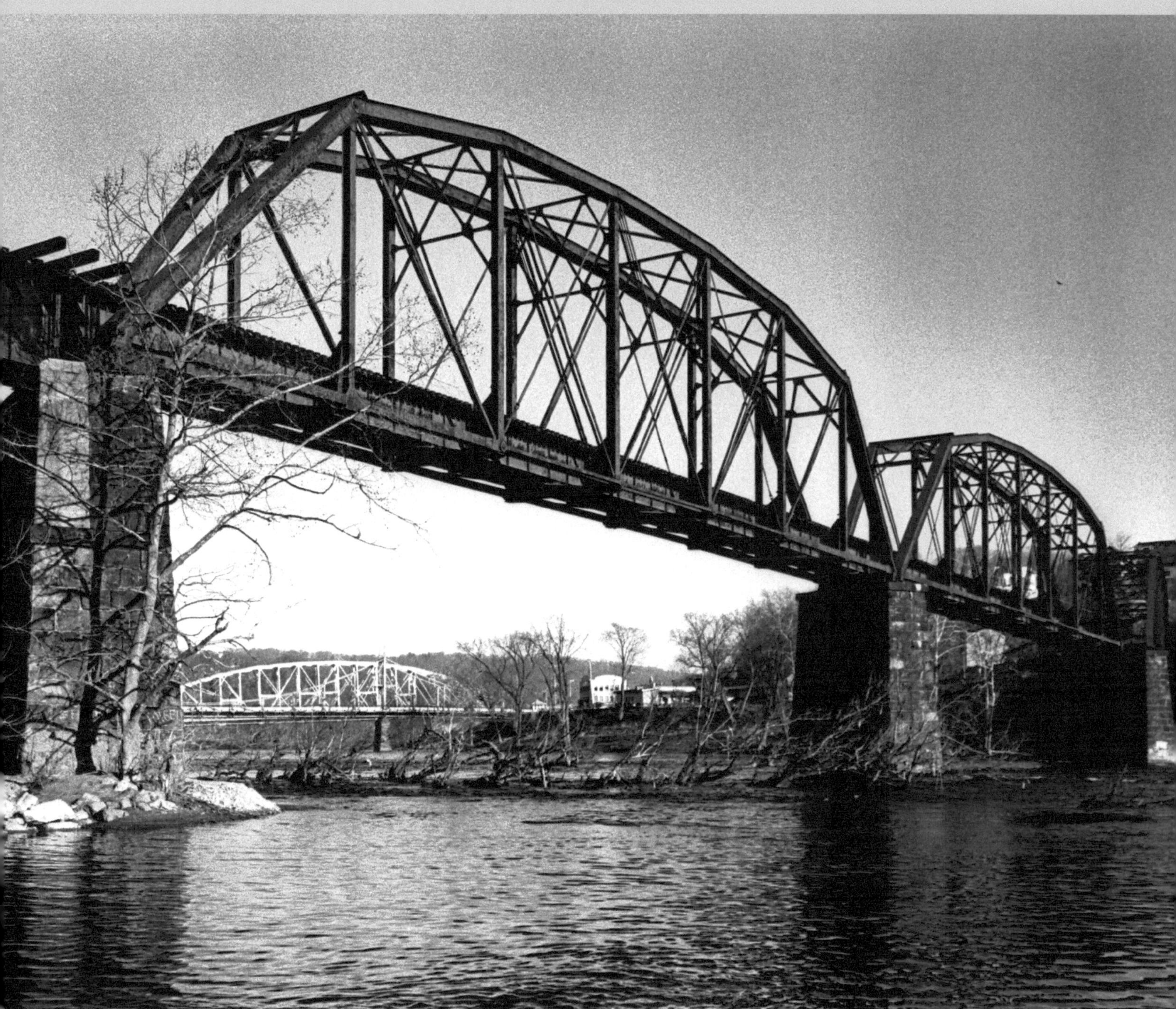

The PA-NJ Turnpike Bridge opened to traffic in 1956, making it a modern bridge by the basic standards in my ***Bridges*** trilogy. The engineering record calls it a *through arch*, which refers to vehicles passing through and under the arched-shaped structure that carries the roadway on suspended vertical cables.

Structurally, it's a *continuous truss in the shape of an arch*, like the Francis Scott Key Bridge (page 23), the US Route 40 Bridge (pages 32+33), and a host of bridges we covered in Volume 1. "Continuous" refers to the way tension and compression forces are shared without interruption as the bridge passes over the piers; there are no breaks or joints as with typical truss designs. They are also mathematically complex expressions that the digital computer has notably enabled recently; it seems most modern-day arches are continuous trusses.

Continuous truss arches are graceful things having a linear elegance like a gentle wrinkle on the earth's horizon. Contrast this with the Tacony-Palmyra Bridges on page 88. Flip the pages back and forth and discern the radical difference between the two types of arches; they couldn't be more distinct. I've dubbed the Tacony-Palmyra type a *proper* steel arch, a rare thing we visited on a handful of occasions in Volume 1; Pittsburgh is an excellent place to find them. Proper arches pierce the sky and strike radically against the horizon. They have a singular beauty that breaks sharply with the roadway, the river, and the surrounding countryside; you can't miss them.

Before we proceed, please revisit the "Tacony" inside cover photo. For me, it was a local bridge with many memories attached and is near where we lived for 24 years in Philadelphia.

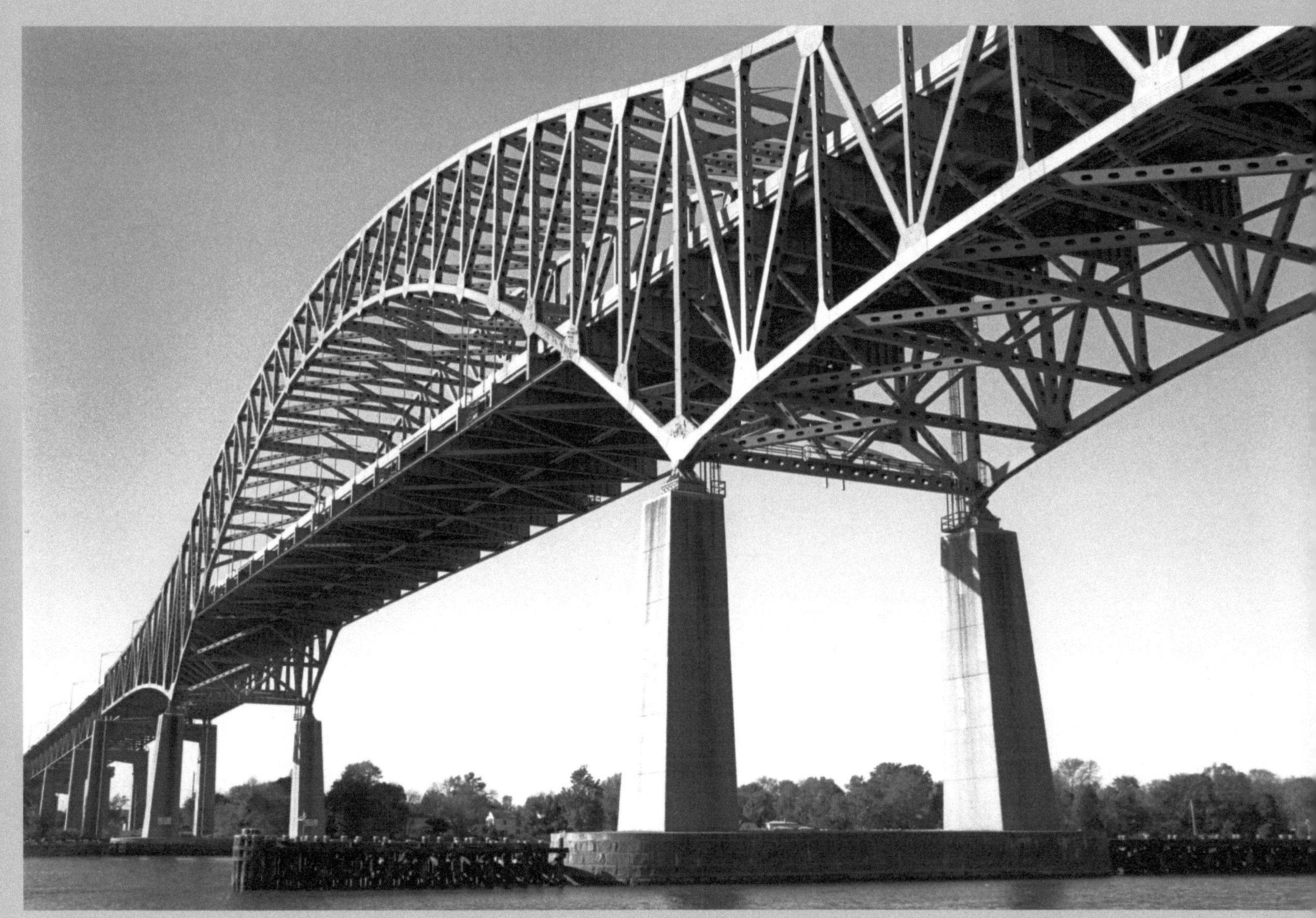

01-6564-27

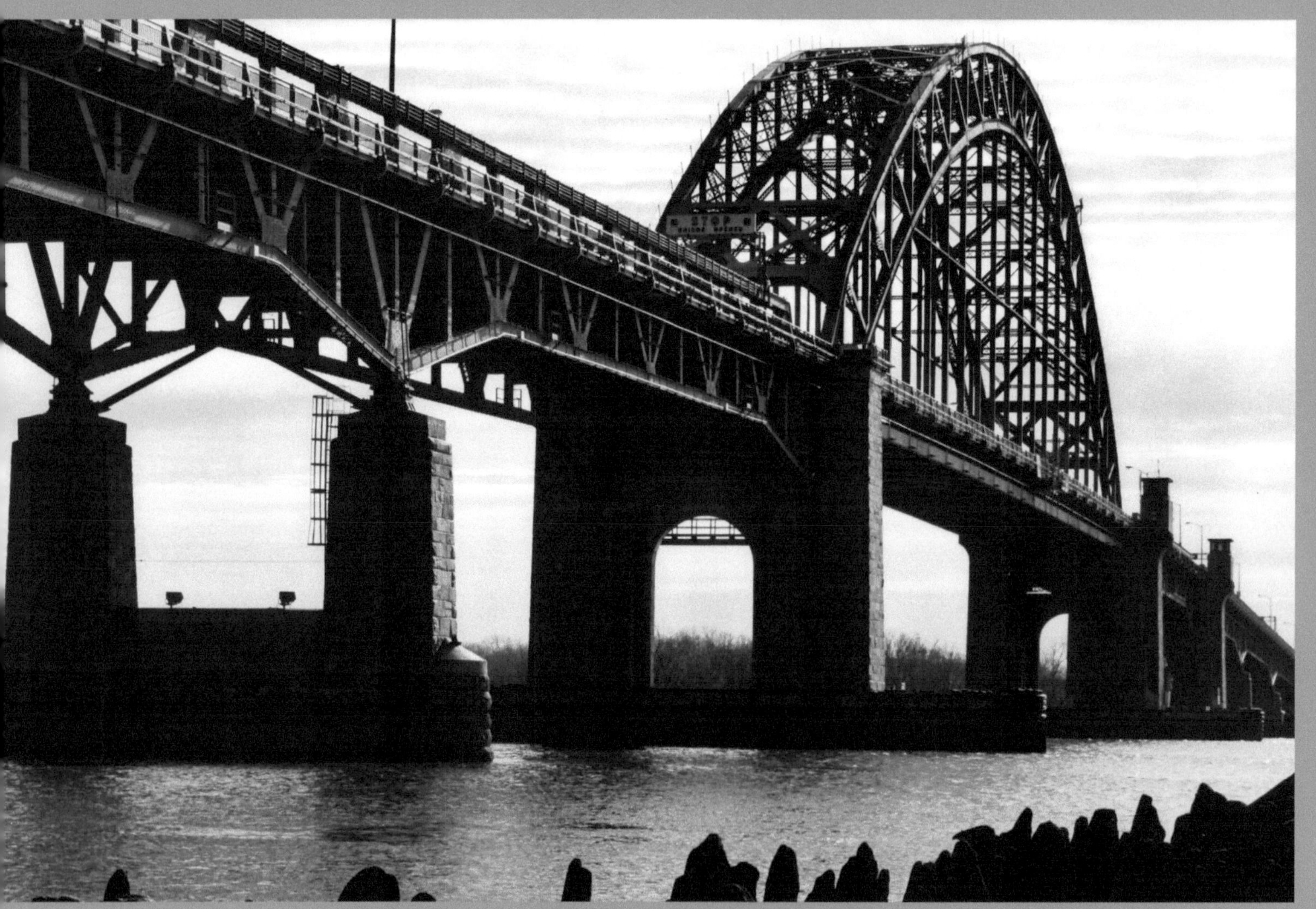


13-4815-26

The Tacony-Palmyra Bridge is a *tied* arch, often called a *bowstring* arch. This design uses the roadway to prevent the two ends of the arch from spreading apart and thus avoids a bridge collapse. The roadway is like the bowstring that pulls the bow into its characteristic "bow" shape; cut the bowstring, and it loses shape, which equals a flattened bridge. The arch and the roadway inside it are a closed unit, a singular structure, placed atop the robust stone piers on either end. The arched assembly is *discontinuous* of the approach spans and shares no structural forces with the rest of the bridge. This fact starkly contrasts the *continuous* truss arch that oozes past the adjacent piers, spreading its structural energy along a more expansive stretch of the entire span.

A proper arch can be identified by its compact appearance and skyward prowess; these things have a stunning and majestic presence. The Tacony-Palmyra Bridge is attributed to Ralph Modjeski, a polish-born American architect and civil engineer. His firm, Modjeski+Masters, is responsible for numerous masterpieces across the United States, including the Ben Franklin Bridge, which we will visit in a few pages.

The view on pages 90+91 is from the New Jersey side and addresses the issue of lighting and how its direction can radically change how something is recorded by the camera. The pronounced rich textures and distinctive design characteristics speak well of the unique instincts of Modjeski and his team. Working in the shadows of steel bridges has been inspirational and humbling as a sculptor who has spent a lifetime practicing a modernist idiom and using bridge design principles.

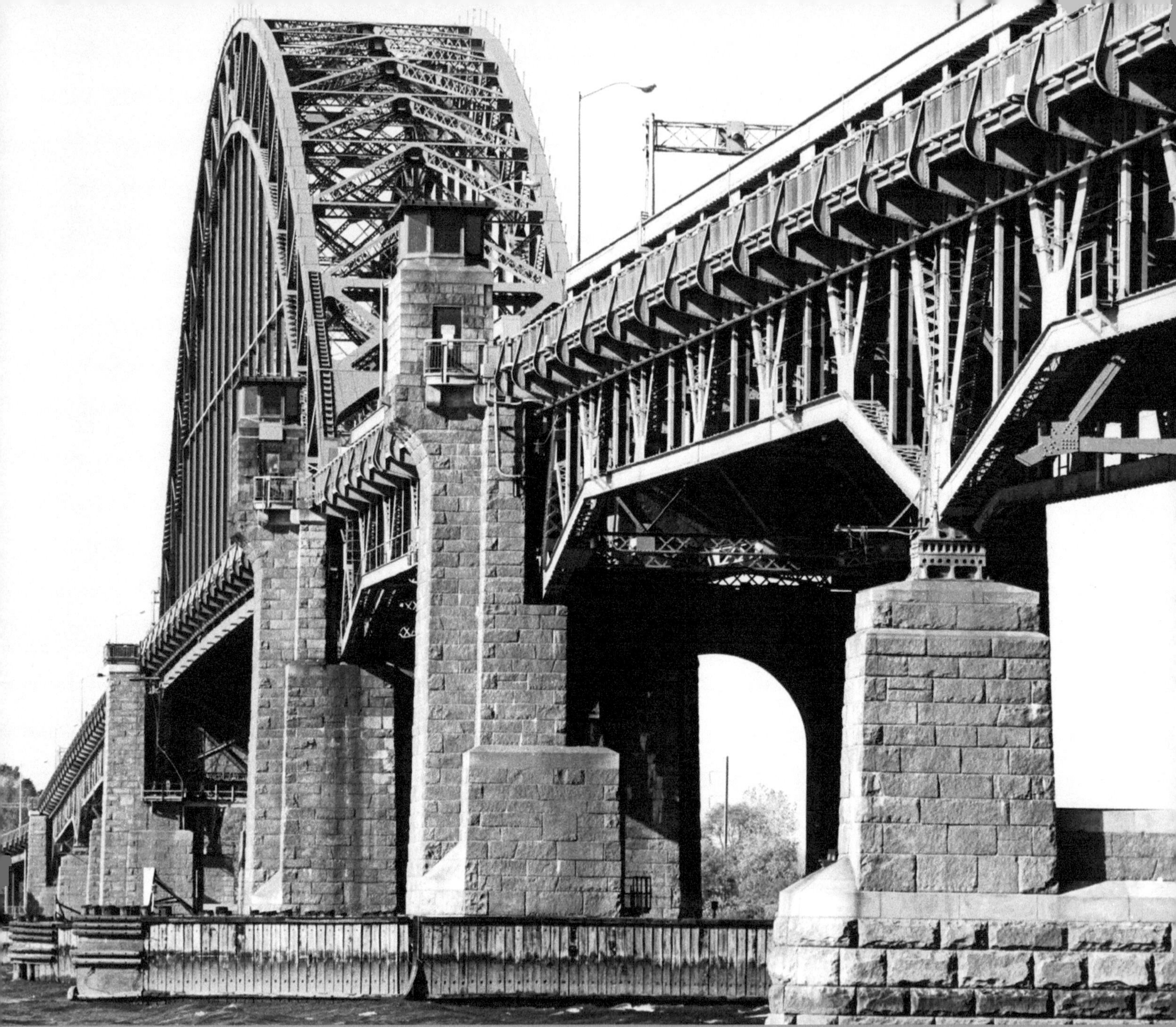

90.

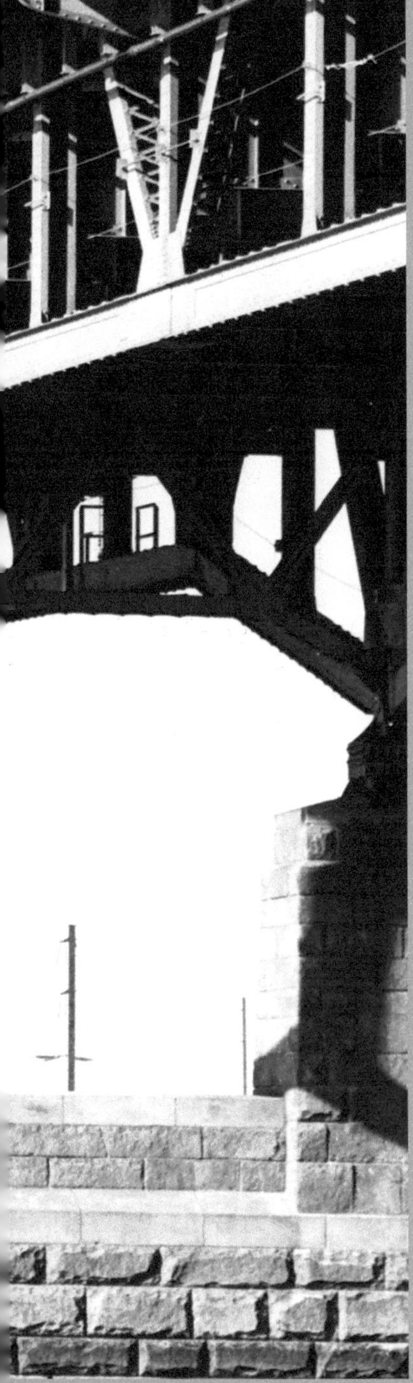

01-6556-34

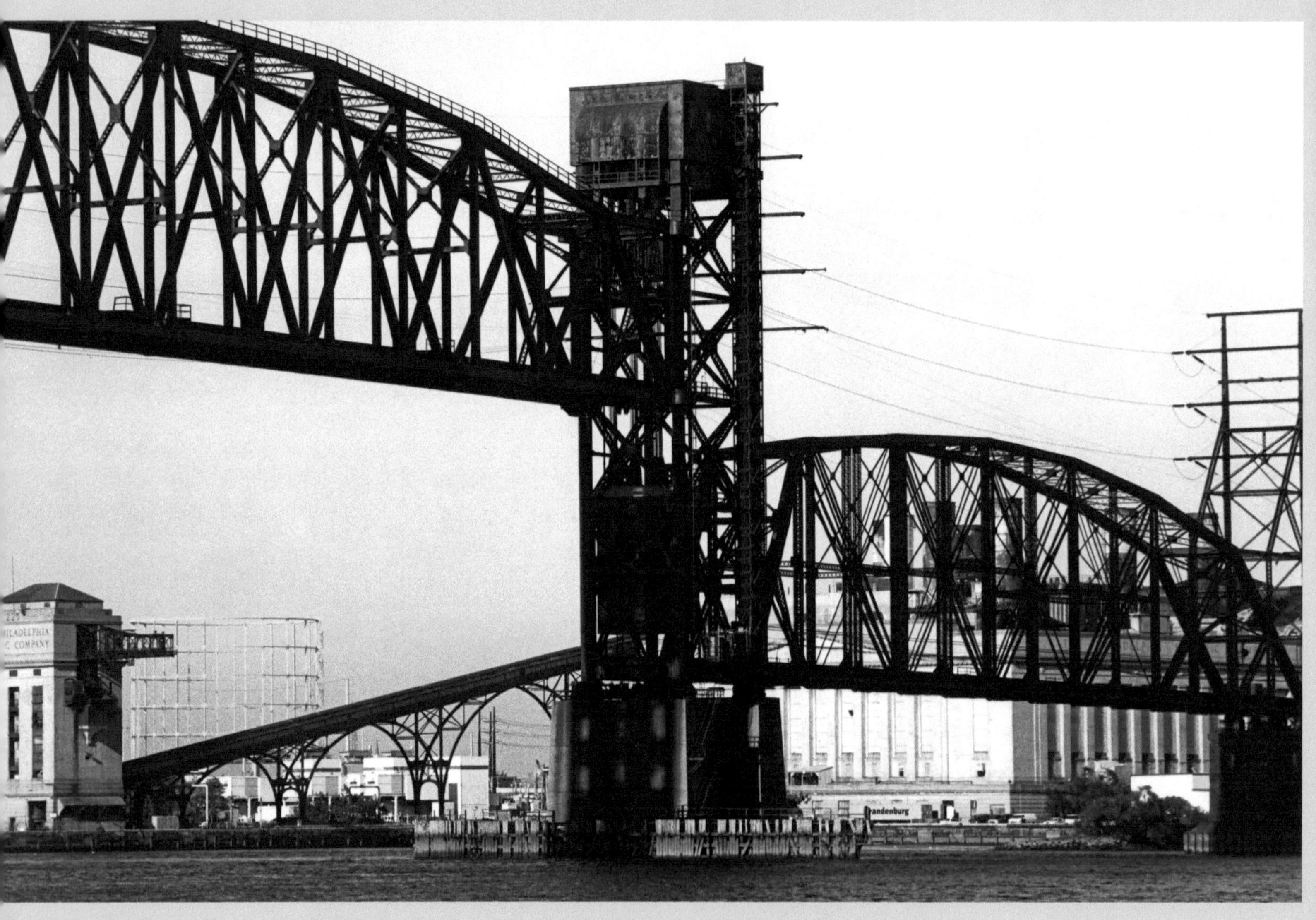

01-6536-18

92.

I could spot the Delair Bridge from the third-floor windows of our Lower Kensington/Fishtown rowhouse; it was a Delaware River landmark for over two decades of driving and bicycling up and down the river ward neighborhoods where I gathered supplies for my busy studio enterprise. The acreage along the river north of Center City was wonderfully desolate. Here I frequented aluminum and steel yards, anodizing factories, tooling supplies, and a lacquer manufacturer where all the blue and white-collar workers were totally batsh#t crazy from breathing the chemical thinners used in the various blends. I never paid the same price for the same product, but it averaged reasonably after many years. I still have a drum of the stuff in my rural studio where I keep the lid tight; it's a good product that compensates for any loss of brain cells. At this point, I won't miss them anyway.

The Delair Bridge was finished in 1896 and was the first span from Philadelphia to New Jersey. It's called a railroad *lift* bridge, but this feature was added in 1960 by replacing the original swing-span drawbridge. The renovation allowed for the passage of larger boats and barges to service the growing transportation needs of the region, especially the increasing demands for electrical power generation and the concomitant appetite for river-transported coal.

The area surrounding the Delair Bridge is solidly industrial, more accurately post-industrial, with endless fields of scrub vegetation growing from abandoned machine-age architecture and riverside docking infrastructure. A conspicuous example is the Richmond Power Station, which appears in the background of all but one of my Delair Bridge photos. The Greek Parthenon is suggested by its Doric pediments and columns molded with thousands of square yards of steel-reinforced concrete. Inside are the dinosaur-like remains of the highest expressions of industrial-age self-confidence. Multiple enormous coal-fired turbines once purred day and night, electrifying Philadelphia's endless acres of factories and workshops. Today, the entire area is a dry bed; I would go bird-watching where blue-aproned men once stood behind lathes and milling machines.

I have a lathe and milling machine in my studio, vintage items bought pre-owned from a dealer who distributed these things to an invisible new generation of operators. I make sculptures with mine. I don't know where the other ones go. He told me many of these things end up in Mexico, where skilled labor is understood and appreciated and, heaven forbid, taught.

I used to purchase tooling for my machines in the Bridesburg neighborhood, near the Frankford Arsenal, where they designed and manufactured the complex aerial bomb sights used in WWII. Here was the Silicon Valley of the now defunct analog age, where machine shops once lined the streets, and food trucks and corner stores sold lunch to lines of workers. I would go to Tocaro Machinery Company every month and pick up something I needed. Back then, I was a self-taught machinist and knew nothing about what I was buying, but Tocaro always knew what I needed and had it in stock. Throughout the entire 24 years I went to his shop, I never once saw another customer. He closed his doors a few years after we moved.

01-6531-32



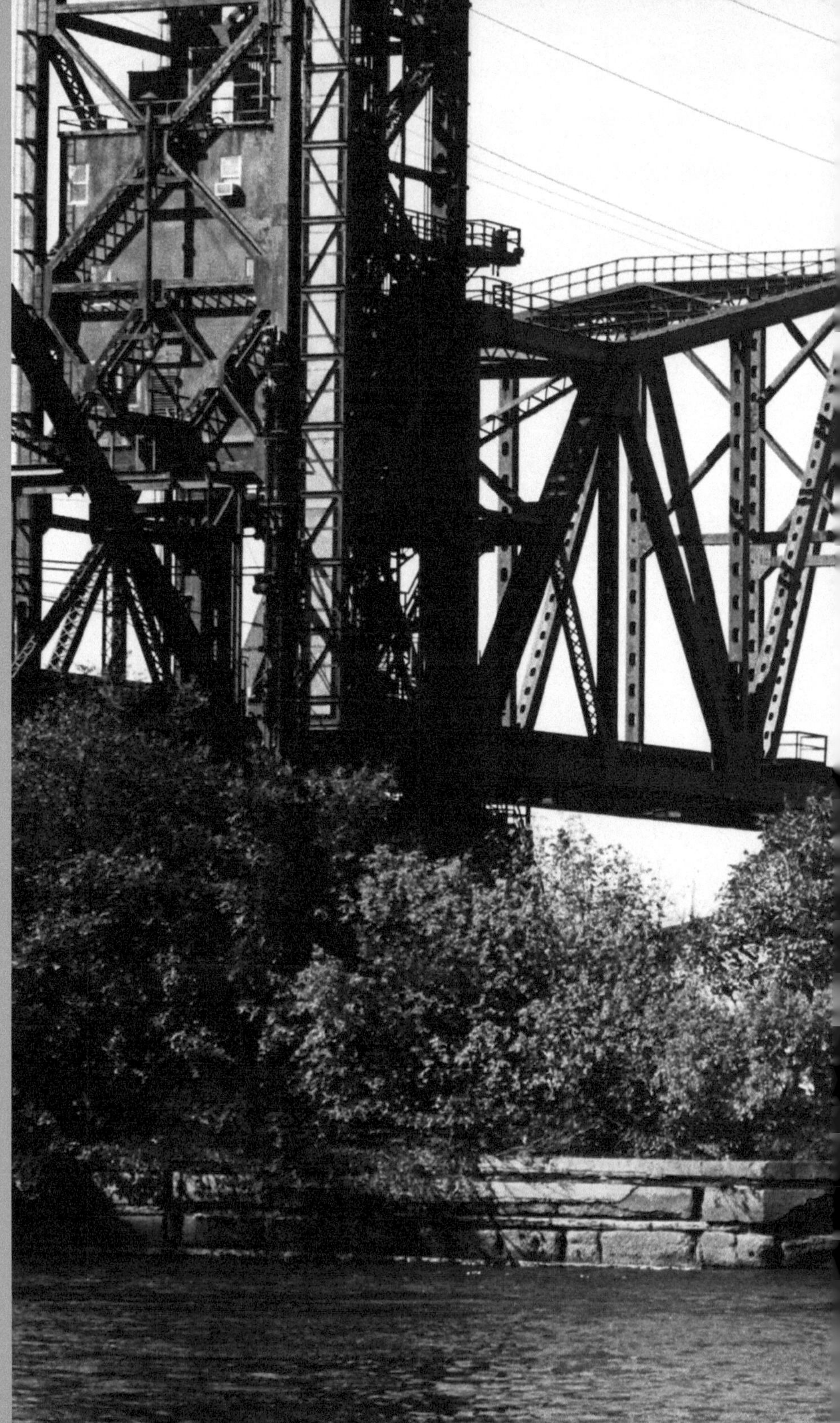

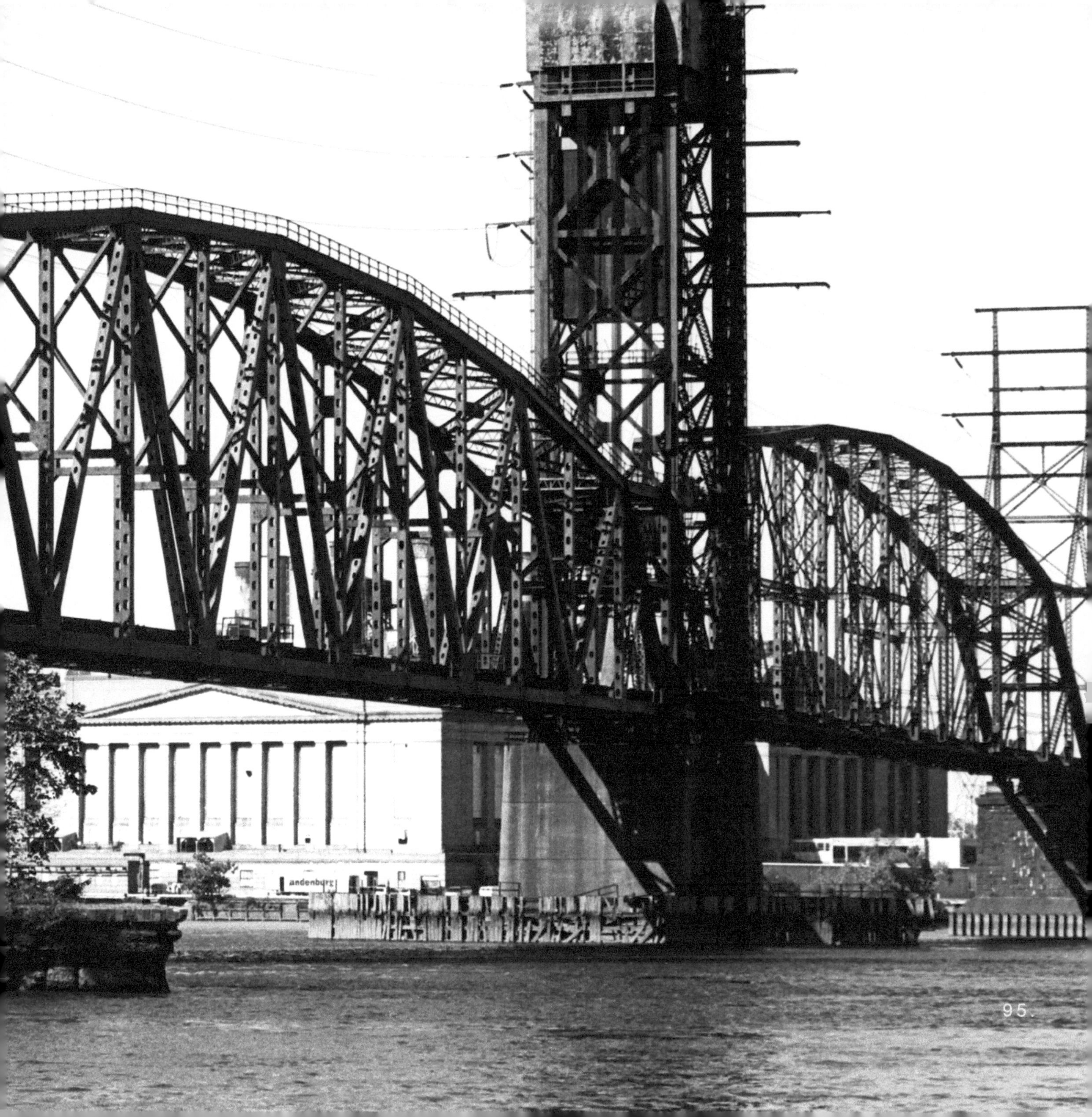
andenburg

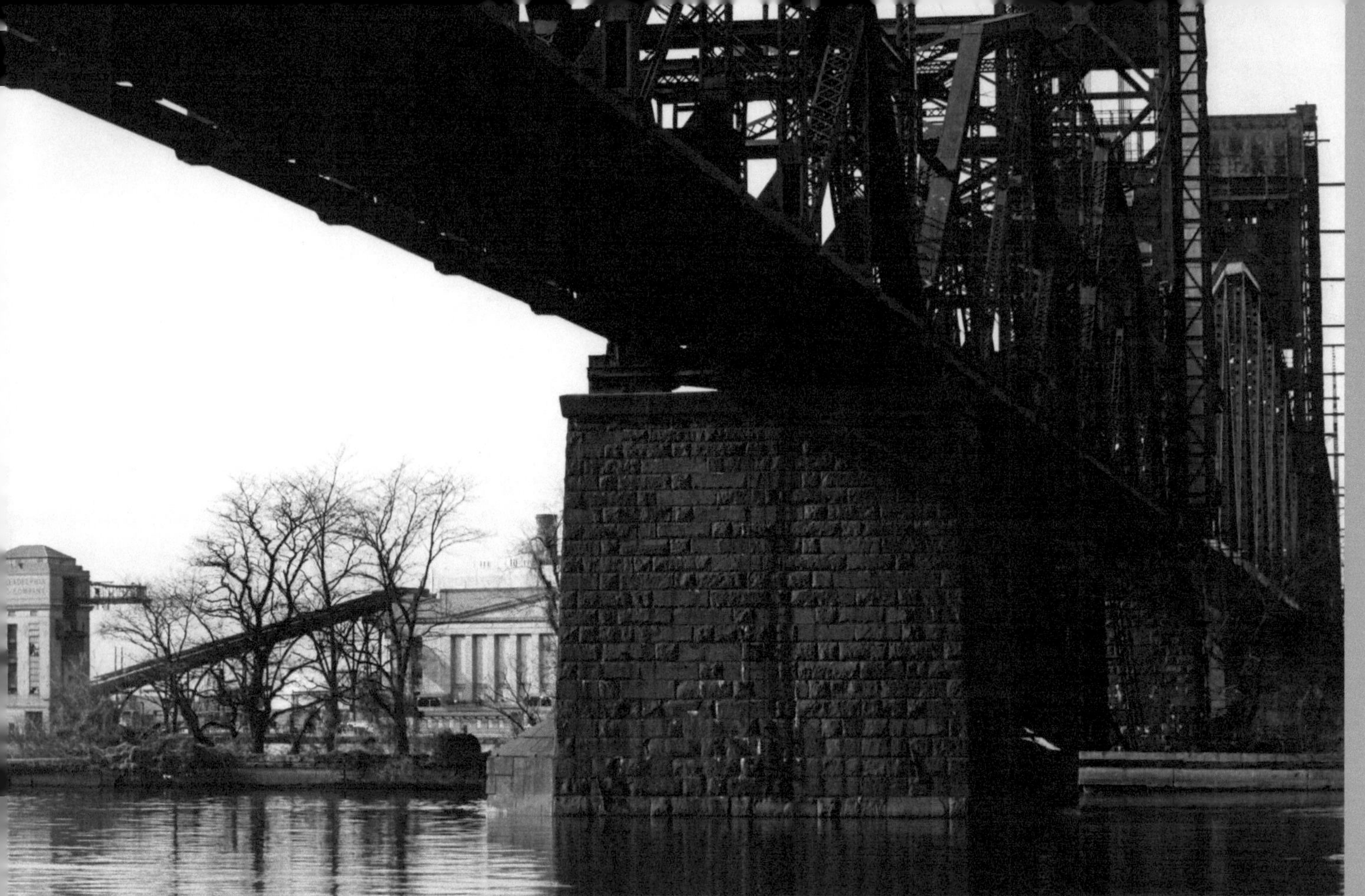

01-3657-07

01-3651-25

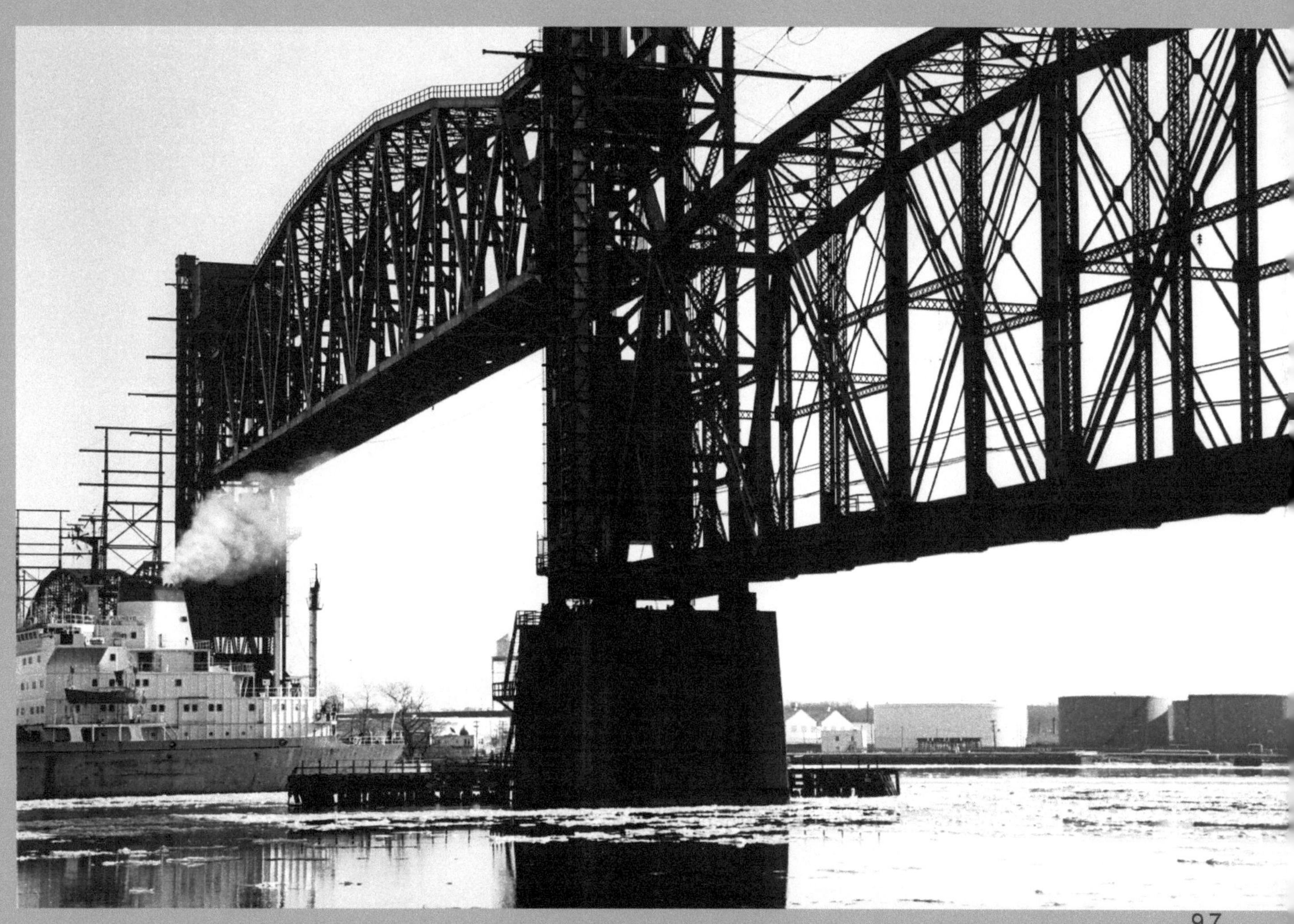

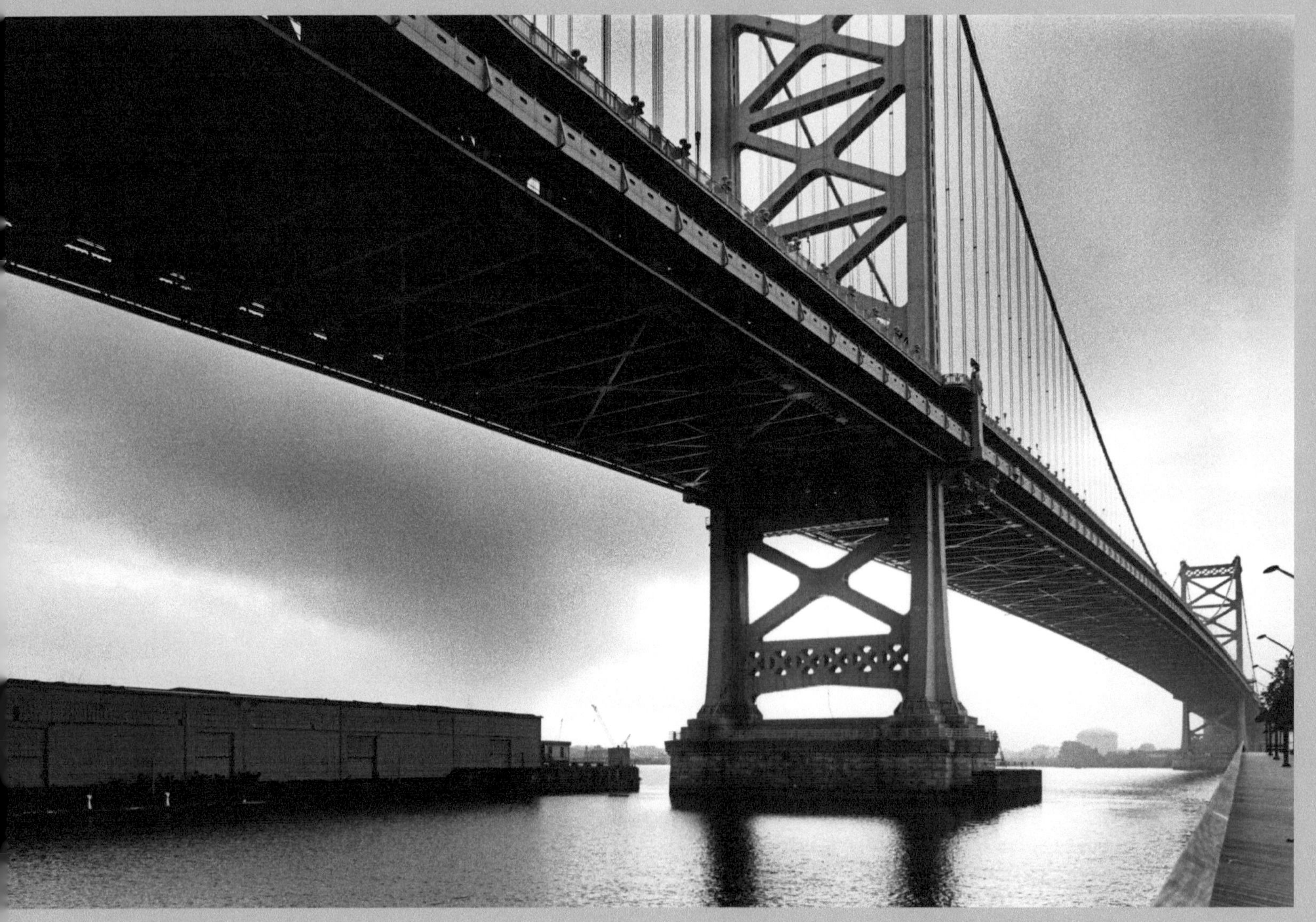

12-4676-04

The glorious Ben Franklin Bridge is our last major stop on our Mid-Atlantic journey. It came from the desk of Ralph Modjeski, introduced in our discussion about the Tacony-Palmyra Bridge on page 89, and stands as the apotheosis of American machine-age design. Gratefully, it is well appreciated and maintained by the transportation authorities and, alongside the Liberty Bell, is Philadelphia's premier landmark and civic symbol. I could see the bridge from our rowhouse back windows and took it for granted. I never bothered to get a complete picture from the New Jersey side with Center City in the background, thus missing the postcard view that some may have expected. No worries, my images captured the majesty and some design details that made the bridge prized.

Modjeski's modernism is close to perfect. The demands of structural logic are uppermost in designing a safe bridge where the form is religiously determined and constrained by function. This is the purview of the civil engineer, and Modjeski wasn't unique in mastering the role. Where he stands out, in my estimation, is his architectural skill. He walked past the engineer's boundaries with profound genius by adding grace in volume and line without resorting to superfluous ornamentation; function constrained his forms, yet a poet's eye informed their articulation without adding anything. This describes the minimalist and visual puritanism that made Modernism an American achievement yet relied on Europeans to bring it into conscious awareness and express it as a particular school of design.

The photos on pages 100 through 103 focus on details, and Modjeski and his design team had it right, all the way down to the rivets. Here was High Modernism, design according to the discipline of numbers, as applied on a drawing board under an incandescent light bulb, before technology could outrun the human spirit. It was a moment of perfect balance that lingered into the mid-20th Century and began to be corrupted under the noise of a grasping, impatient culture lost in fogs of mass communication and marketing. Someone once said, "The modern world makes people mentally ill." Like the Uroboros, we may be destined to eat ourselves, starting at the tail. We can only hope this ancient symbol of renewal still carries meaning.

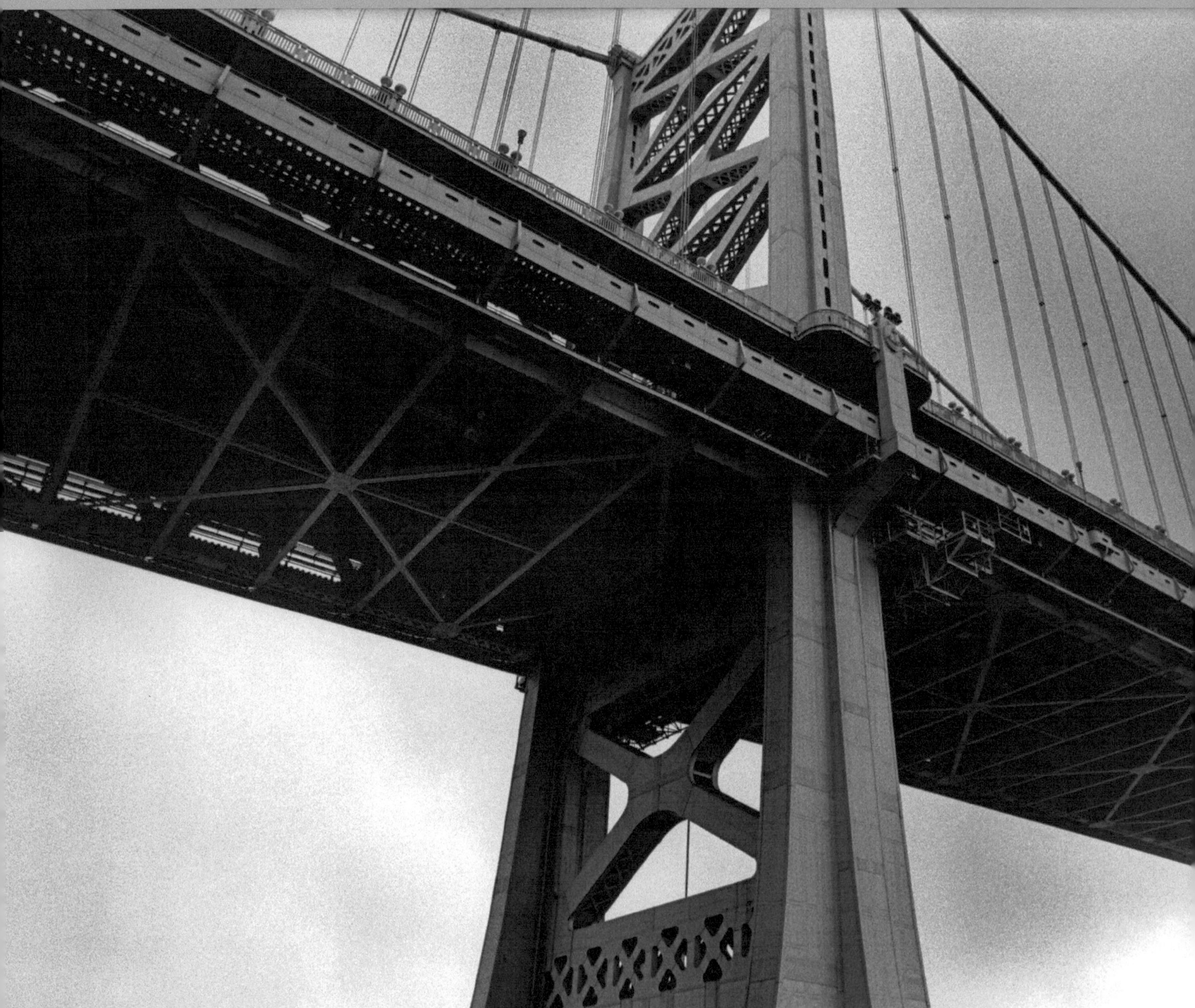

100.

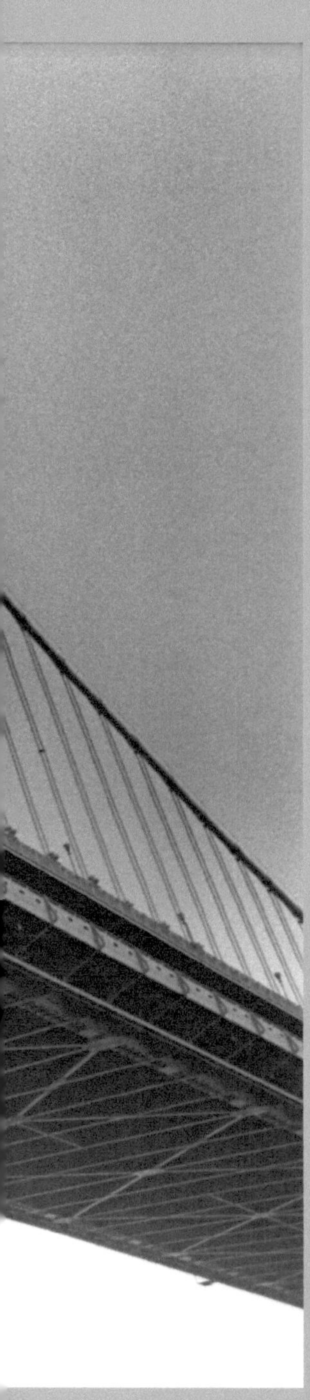

12-4676-29

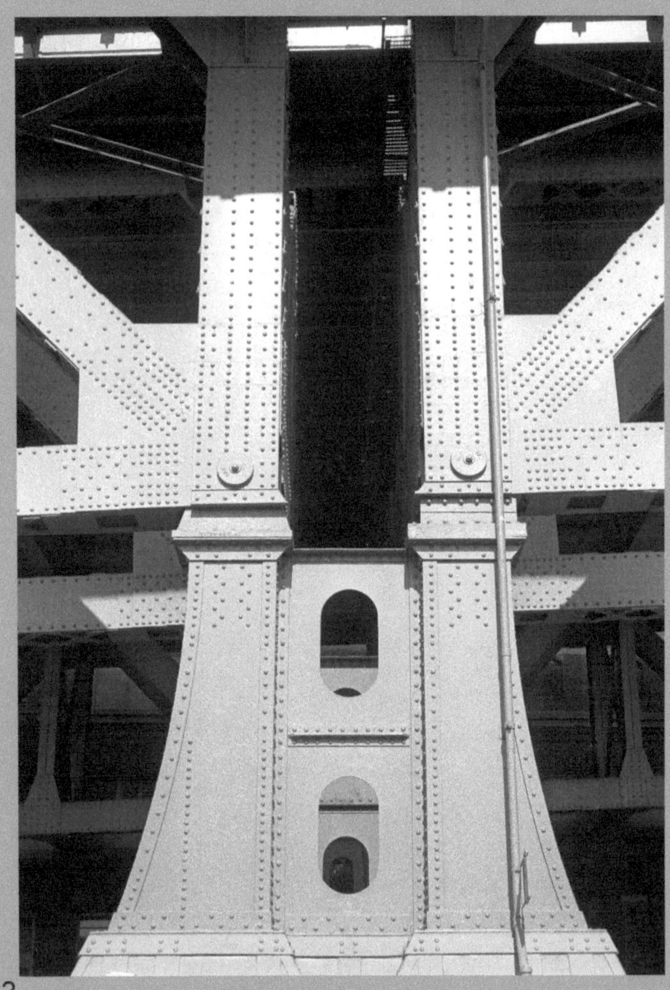

91-0003-08

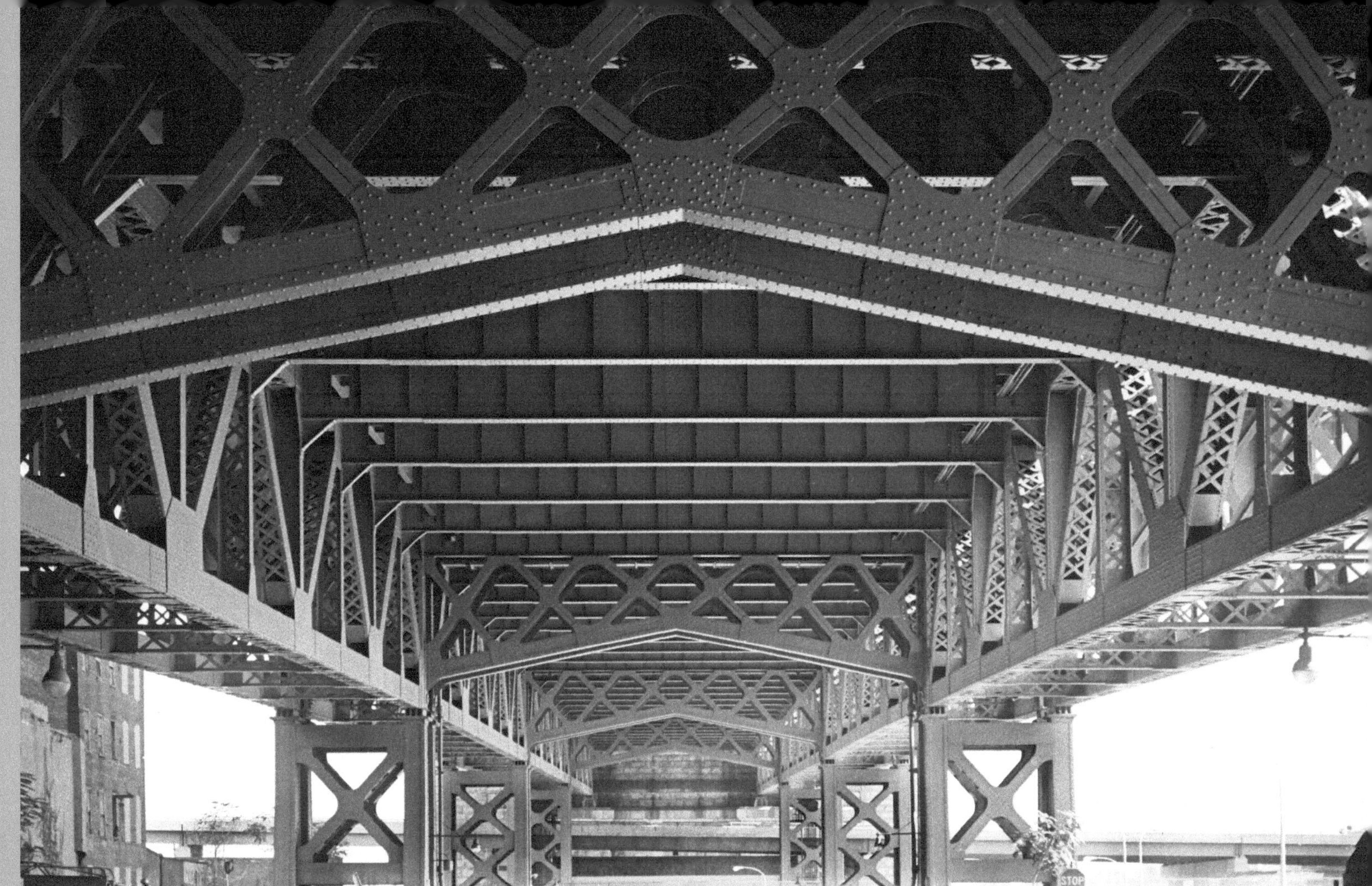


91-0002-20

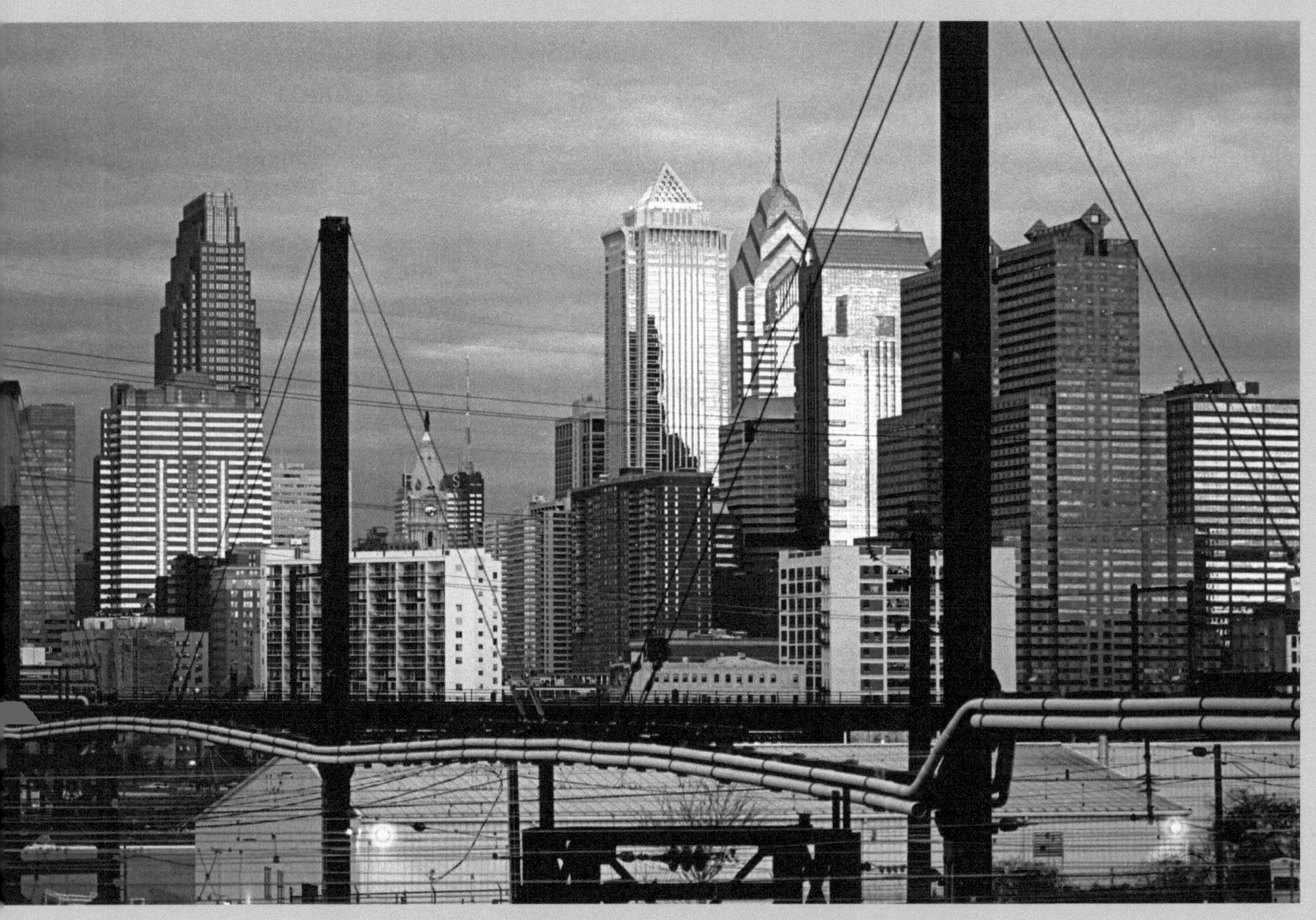

02-6807-32

The photograph on page 104 shows a nameless span carrying a PVC pipeline over a railroad yard in West Philly. What's inside the pipe? I don't know. Two tubes are bundled together, and one is disconnected at the bend. My guess there use is related to something electrical. The span type is called a cable-stayed bridge and is the dominant concept used in many bridges built in recent times. I included the picture to signify a farewell to my former hometown and a reminder of how the skyline looked back in 2002; it's built up a lot since then. Joan and I moved there in our 20s and cut teeth in its galleries, institutions, and artist co-ops for over two decades. There are more than a few stories to tell, and I hope to share them with you in a future volume. Friends have encouraged us to write autobiographies, claiming they will read them when available.

Flipping to the next page shows us another nameless bridge, cut in half and abandoned when they built Interstate 80 across Pennsylvania. It's an antique railroad viaduct probably built in the middle of the 19th Century. I often come across abandoned railroad beds when exploring my adopted state; at one time, it had a veritable spider's web of rail lines. Today, what's left of them are occasional piles of decaying railroad ties sliding down the sides of manmade berms and stone outcrops. Sometimes, the mysterious telegraph poles that lined track beds are still present, with intact and running powerlines carrying electricity for purposes unknown to me. These things appear and disappear like Appalachian ghosts asking us for something.

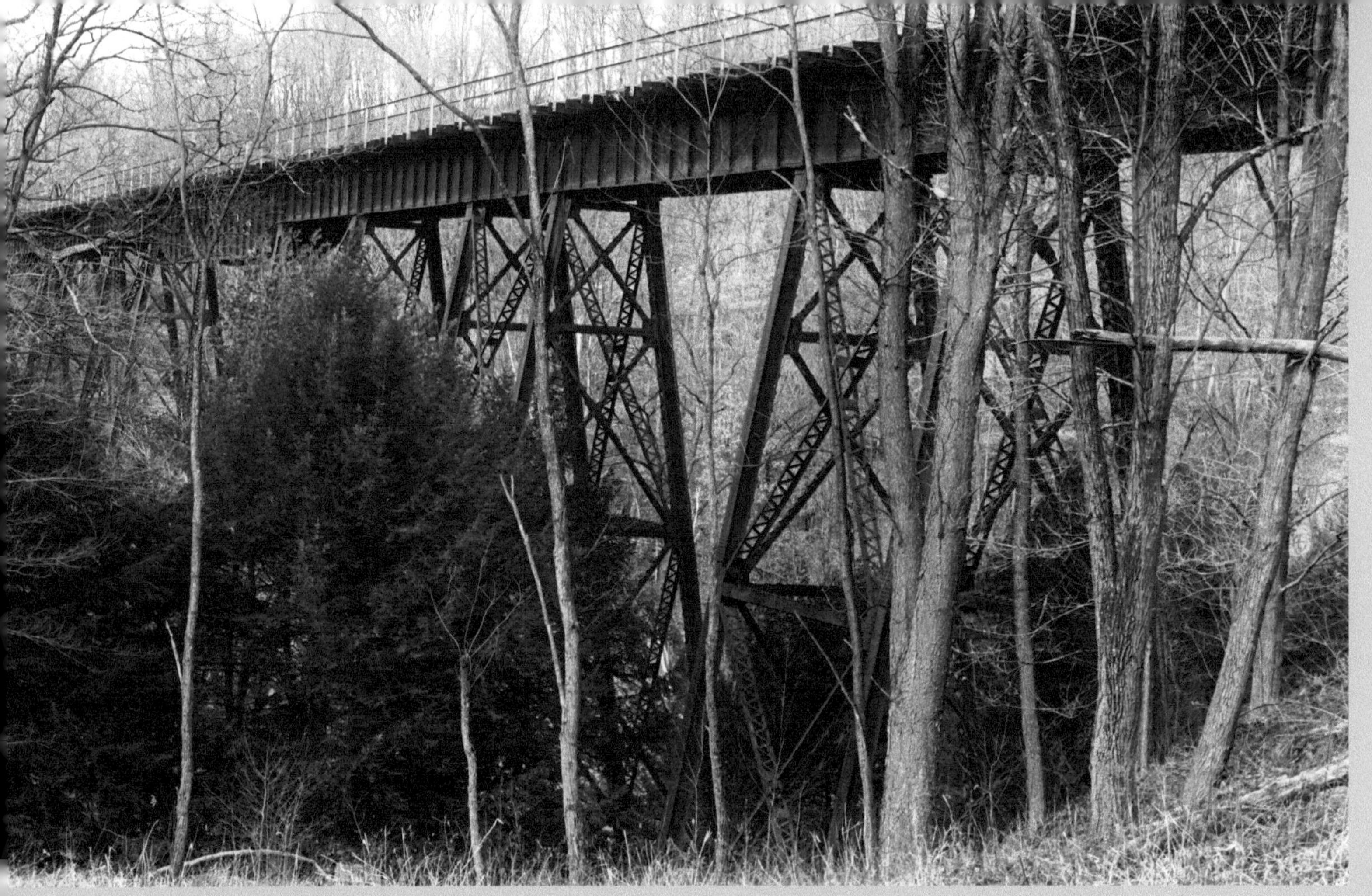

00-2351-02

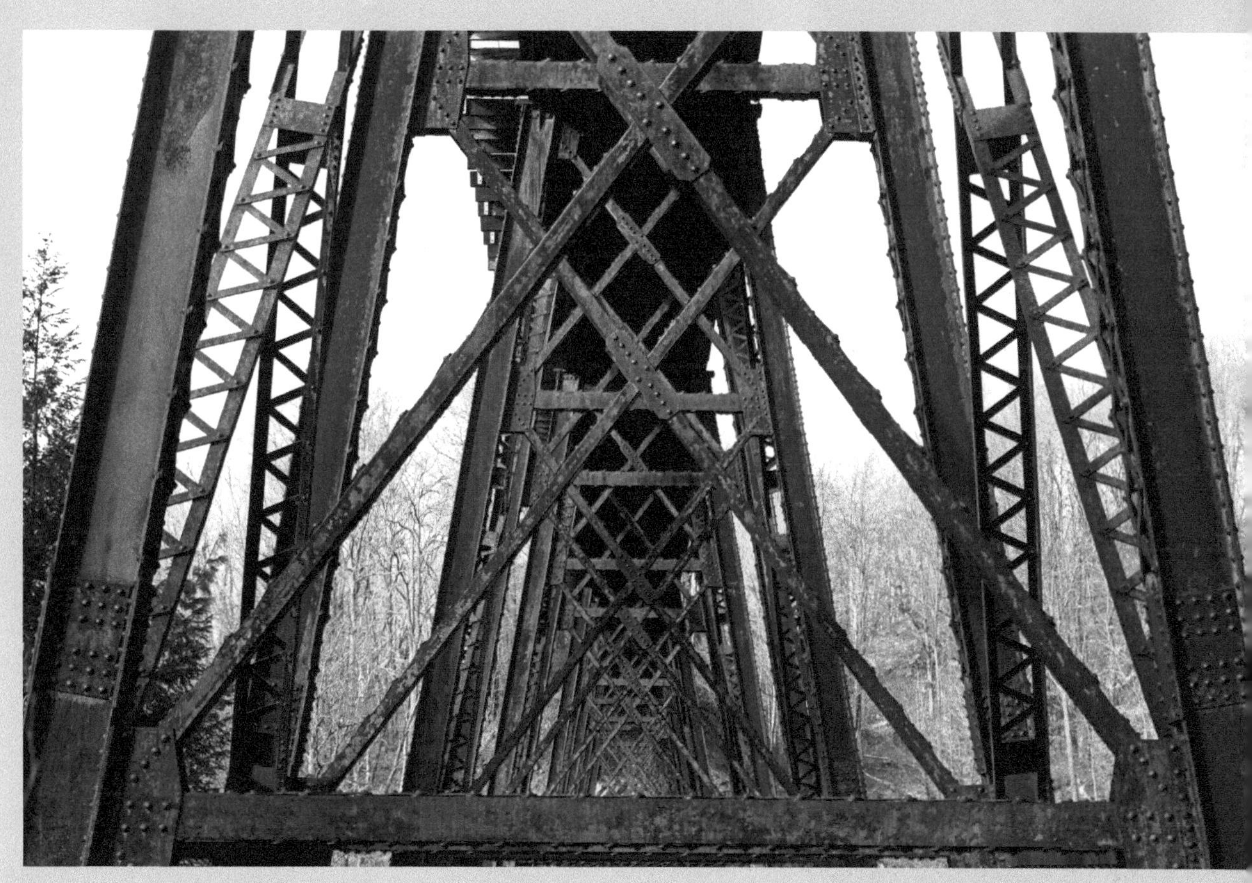

00-2324-28

We've arrived at the end of Volume 2 of ***Bridges***, and my parting bridge photo has no steel of any shape or kind in it. The Starrucca Viaduct illustrates the Old World character of the Mid-Atlantic region with its nod to Roman canal viaducts; its lead stone-mason was an Irish-born immigrant named Thomas Heavey. The Starrucca Viaduct was built in 1848, eight years before Henry Bessemer introduced the decarburizing converter, which made steel available on an industrial scale. Still used for rail transport today, the Starrucca Viaduct was designed and built to exceptionally high standards and can easily compete with any known structure for almost infinite longevity.

Underneath the sky and stone arches are the soil and people of the Appalachian countryside, characterized by the wood-framed house and shadow-laden trees. Modernity abandoned the scene too many years ago to count, but somehow, the people remain.

In Volume 3, we turn our sights westward, past the Ohio Valley, to where the sky opens to the infinite space of the American Midwest and Great Plains. We will watch bridges grow larger and scrape a more expansive horizon as the mood shifts to the New World optimism that characterized the people that followed the sun.

Please join me on the final leg of our adventure through America's steel spans.

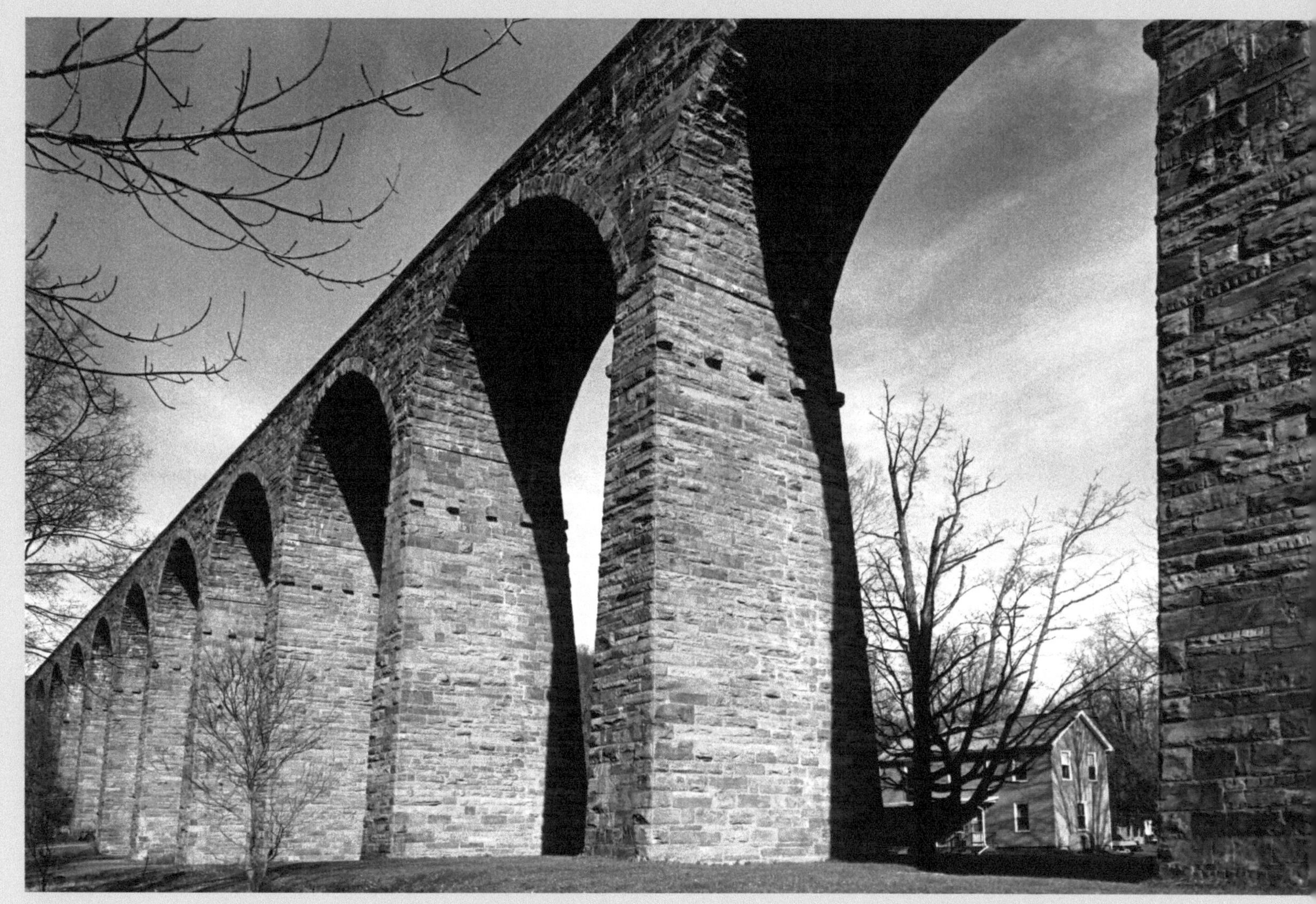

11-4630-27

## Index Volume 2

| | | |
|---|---|---|
| Page 77. | 01-3955-31. | Queensboro Bridge. East River. |
| Page 78. | 14-4834-25. | Neshanic Station Bridge. Raritan River. |
| Pages 80+81. | 14-4834-15. | Neshanic Station Bridge. Raritan River. |
| Page 83. | 12-4641-08. | 3rd Street Railroad Bridge. Lehigh River. |
| Pages 84+85. | 12-4640-08. | Lehigh and Hudson River Valley Railroad Bridge. Delaware River. |
| Page 87. | 01-6564-27. | PA-NJ Turnpike Bridge. Delaware River. |
| Page 88. | 13-4815-26. | Tacony-Palmyra Bridge. Delaware River. |
| Pages 90+91. | 01-6556-34. | Tacony-Palmyra Bridge. Delaware River. |
| Page 92. | 01-6536-18. | Delair Memorial Railroad Bridge. Delaware River. |
| Pages 94+95. | 01-6531-32. | Delair Memorial Railroad Bridge. Delaware River. |
| Page 96. | 01-3657-07. | Delair Memorial Railroad Bridge. Delaware River. |
| Page 97. | 01-3651-25. | Delair Memorial Railroad Bridge. Delaware River. |
| Page 98. | 12-4676-04. | Ben Franklin Bridge. Delaware River. |
| Pages 100+101. | 12-4676-29. | Ben Franklin Bridge. Delaware River. |
| Page 102. | 91-0003-08. | Ben Franklin Bridge. Delaware River. |
| Page 103. | 91-0002-20. | Ben Franklin Bridge. Delaware River. |
| Page 104. | 02-6807-32. | Cable-stayed Pipeline Bridge. |
| Page 106. | 00-2351-02. | Abandoned Railroad Viaduct. |
| Page 107. | 00-2324-28. | Abandoned Railroad Viaduct. |
| Page 109. | 11-4630-27. | Starrucca Viaduct. Starrucca Creek. |

www.ingramcontent.com/pod-product-compliance
Lightning Source LLC
LaVergne TN
LVHW070214110826
845147LV00003B/576